THE GOSPEL ACCORDING TO
THE OLD TESTAMENT

*A series of studies on the lives
of Old Testament characters, written for
laypeople and pastors, and designed to
encourage Christ-centered reading, teaching,
and preaching of the Old Testament*

IAIN M. DUGUID
Series Editor

FROM BONDAGE TO LIBERTY

THE GOSPEL ACCORDING TO

MOSES

ANTHONY T. SELVAGGIO

P&R
PUBLISHING
P.O. BOX 817 • PHILLIPSBURG • NEW JERSEY 08865-0817

978-1-59638-640-2 (pbk)
978-1-59638-641-9 (ePub)
978-1-59638-642-6 (Mobi)

Printed in the United States of America

Library of Congress Cataloging-in-Publication Data

Selvaggio, Anthony T.
  From bondage to liberty : the Gospel according to Moses / Anthony T. Selvaggio.
      pages cm. -- (The Gospel according to the Old Testament)
  Includes bibliographical references and index.
  ISBN 978-1-59638-640-2 (pbk.)
  1. Bible. Exodus--Criticism, interpretation, etc. 2. Moses (Biblical leader) 3. Exodus, The. 4. Bible. Exodus--Relation to the New Testament. 5. Bible. New Testament--Relation to Exodus. 6. Typology (Theology) I. Title.
  BS1245.52.S45 2013
  222'.1206--dc23
                                                    2013010513

To my daughter, Katie,
through whom I have learned so much
about God's providence and love

and

To the Rev. Dr. James D. Carson,
whose deep love for Jesus Christ and his church
continues to inspire and challenge me

CONTENTS

FOREWORD

The New Testament is in the Old concealed;
the Old Testament is in the New revealed.
—Augustine

Concerning this salvation, the prophets who prophesied about the grace that was to be yours searched and inquired carefully, inquiring what person or time the Spirit of Christ in them was indicating when he predicted the sufferings of Christ and the subsequent glories. It was revealed to them that they were serving not themselves but you, in the things that have now been announced to you through those who preached the good news to you by the Holy Spirit sent from heaven, things into which angels long to look. (1 Peter 1:10–12 ESV)

"Moreover, some women of our company amazed us. They were at the tomb early in the morning, and when they did not find his body, they came back saying that they had even seen a vision of angels, who said that he was alive. Some of those who were with us went to the tomb and found it just as the women had said, but him they did not see." And he said to them, "O foolish ones, and slow of heart to believe all that the prophets have spoken! Was it not necessary that the Christ should suffer these things and enter into his glory?" And beginning with Moses and all the Prophets, he interpreted to them

in all the Scriptures the things concerning himself.
(Luke 24:22–27 ESV)

The prophets searched. Angels longed to see. And the disciples didn't understand. But Moses, the Prophets, and all the Old Testament Scriptures had spoken about it—that Jesus would come, suffer, and then be glorified. God began to tell a story in the Old Testament, the ending of which the audience eagerly anticipated. But the Old Testament audience was left hanging. The plot was laid out, but the climax was delayed. The unfinished story begged for an ending. In Christ, God has provided the climax to the Old Testament story. Jesus did not arrive unannounced; his coming was declared *in advance* in the Old Testament—not just in explicit prophecies of the Messiah, but also by means of the stories of all the events, characters, and circumstances in the Old Testament. God was telling a larger, overarching, unified story. From the account of creation in Genesis to the final stories of the return from exile, God progressively unfolded his plan of salvation. And the Old Testament account of that plan always pointed in some way to Christ.

AIMS OF THIS SERIES

The Gospel According to the Old Testament series was begun by my former professors, Tremper Longman and Al Groves, to whom I owe an enormous personal debt of gratitude. I learned from them a great deal about how to recognize the gospel in the Old Testament. I share their deep conviction that the Bible, both Old and New Testaments, is a unified revelation of God and that its thematic unity is found in Christ. This series of studies will continue to pursue their initial aims:

- to lay out the pervasiveness of the revelation of Christ in the Old Testament

- to promote a Christ-centered reading of the Old Testament
- to encourage Christ-centered preaching and teaching from the Old Testament

These volumes are written primarily for pastors and laypeople, not scholars. They are designed in the first instance to serve the church, not the academy.

My hope and prayer remain the same as Tremper and Al's: that this series will continue to encourage the revival of interest in the Old Testament as a book that constantly points forward to Jesus Christ, to his sufferings and the glories that would follow.

IAIN M. DUGUID

ACKNOWLEDGMENTS

One of the great joys of writing a book is the creative aspects of the endeavor. Engaging in creative labors is a way, analogically, to explore what it means to be created in the image of God. God is the Creator of all things, and he made us to be "creators" of sorts. Of course, there is a massive distinction between God's creative work and our own. First, God created all things out of nothing, and we create only in a subsidiary manner with preexisting matter. Second, God created without the aid of human beings, whereas our creative endeavors are nearly always dependent on a community of persons. This is certainly true in my own experience and in the case of this book. Accordingly, I wish to acknowledge the contributions of others in this creative work.

First, I want to thank Iain Duguid, the editor of this series and the one who reached out to me with the opportunity to contribute to it. I first met Iain when I was pastoring in western Pennsylvania. I entreated him to come to my church and teach our people. He came and opened the truth of the gospel in the Old Testament in powerful and memorable ways. I can't remember most of my own sermons, but I recall distinctly Iain's winsome and deep presentations. I also profited greatly from one of Iain's contributions to this series. I relied heavily on his volume dealing with the life of Abraham when I was teaching through Genesis. In that volume, Iain marvelously wove together a Christ-centered interpretation of Abraham while simultaneously doing justice to the ethical implications of Abraham's life and actions within the historical milieu in which he lived. I have found similar richness in every other volume penned by Iain, and I am pleased to acknowledge that he has made me a more effective communicator of the Old Testament. But I also wish to give my thanks to Iain for his assistance in editing this manuscript. He provided me with challenging and encouraging comments that vastly improved this creative effort.

Second, I wish to give thanks to others who contributed to this work. I am grateful to all those who reviewed the manuscript and offered endorsements of it. These men have all been very generous with their limited time. I want to particularly thank Dennis Johnson, of Westminster Theological Seminary in California, for his in-depth reading of the manuscript and his helpful comments, which I relied on to improve this book. I also wish to thank the good folks at P&R Publishing for granting me the opportunity to partner with them once again. They do yeoman work in continuing a legacy of producing solid Christian books in the Reformed tradition. Particularly noteworthy are the contributions of John J. Hughes and Rick Matt, each of whom polished this work in significant ways.

Third, I want to give thanks to the people to whom I have preached, pastored, and taught over the years. They have all contributed to this work through their friendships, sufferings, and joys. We are shaped in many ways by those who surround us, and that is certainly true in my case. Of course, the most profound of these personal human relationships is my relationship with my wife, Michelle, and my children, Katie and James. They have shaped me, humbled me, and helped me in this endeavor in innumerable ways.

Finally, I wish to give thanks to my Lord and Savior, Jesus Christ. He has empowered me to create and provided me with the privilege of being a vessel in his service. Although life has taken me on interesting and varied paths, the greatest vocational pleasure that I continue to experience is being used as a bullhorn to proclaim the good news of Jesus Christ. It is my hope that this book will also be used to communicate that inextinguishable, immutable, glorious truth.

INTRODUCTION

A Faithful Servant in God's House

I n the United States we refer to the three major auto-
mobile producers, General Motors, Ford, and Chrysler,
as the "Big Three." When it comes to Old Testament
studies, we can also argue that there is a "Big Three." The
"Big Three" figures of the Old Testament are Abraham,
David, and, the focus of this book, Moses.

It is difficult to overestimate the importance of Moses to
the unfolding of God's plan of salvation. Arguably, Moses
is the most significant Old Testament figure because of
his unique role as mediator of the old covenant. Abraham
and David were significant covenant figures, but, in old
covenant terms, only Moses could claim the role as God's
mediator. In this sense, Moses is the only parallel to Jesus
Christ, who is the mediator of a new and better covenant.
The great Reformed biblical theologian Geerhardus Vos, in
acknowledgment of Moses' vital and unique role in God's
plan, stated that Moses "may be fitly called the redeemer
of the Old Testament."[1] This book will explore the life of
this unparalleled Old Testament figure and how God used
him to reveal and foreshadow the work of Jesus Christ.

The heart of Moses' story is contained in the book
of Exodus. Yes, his story extends to Leviticus, Numbers,
and Deuteronomy, but the heart of his mediatorial and
prophetic work, as well as his personal biography, is to
be found within the pages of the book of Exodus. Accordingly, it will be helpful to have some sense of the structure

and purpose of Exodus and its influence on the entirety of God's written revelation.

EXODUS: THE BOOK

Exodus is both a book and an event. As a book, Exodus is situated among the first five books of the Old Testament, referred to cumulatively as the Pentateuch. This means that Exodus is intimately connected to the book of Genesis, which immediately precedes it. In fact, Exodus should be seen as a continuation of the Genesis story, much like the book of Acts should be viewed as a continuation of the Gospel accounts in the New Testament. Although a significant amount of time has elapsed between the end of Genesis and the beginning of Exodus, Exodus essentially tells the story of the fulfillment of parts of the Abrahamic covenant. When God shared his covenant with Abraham, he informed Abraham of the bondage his descendants would face in Egypt and how God would liberate them from this bondage (Gen. 12:1–3, 5, 17). The book of Exodus details this bondage and demonstrates God's faithfulness in liberating his people and fulfilling his covenant promises to Abraham.

The structure of the book of Exodus is relatively simple. It can be divided into three parts. First, there is the story of Israel's bondage in Egypt and its subsequent deliverance by the power of God mediated through his servant Moses (Ex. 1:1–13:16). In this first part of the book we learn a great deal about Moses' own life and personal transformation. We see God working in the heart of Moses to make him a worthy servant and preparing him for his role as mediator. The second part of the book of Exodus deals with the wilderness wanderings of God's people as they migrate to the land of promise (Ex. 13:17–18:27). During this time we learn a great deal about the nature of human sin and the sufficiency of God. Finally, in the third part of Exodus, we zoom in on Israel at Mount Sinai (Ex. 19:1–40:38). During this final part of Exodus two major events occur—the giving of the law (the Ten Commandments) and the establishment of the Tabernacle.

Though the entirety of this book is monumental in its importance to the rest of redemptive history, the actual exodus event is what casts the greatest shadow upon the rest of God's redemptive revelation.

EXODUS: THE EVENT

God's delivering of his people from bondage in Egypt is the most significant redemptive event of the Old Testament. The exodus creates a paradigm, a type, of the redemptive work of God, and it reveals the basic status of humanity. Due to the fall, humanity is in bondage to sin, much like the Israelites were in bondage to the Egyptians. We are, apart from Christ, in slavery to sin whether we are aware of it or not. The only way to move from bondage to liberation is for God to intervene. God did that in the exodus by using a human mediator—Moses. In the New Testament, of course, we learn that God orchestrates the ultimate deliverance from bondage to sin through the mediatorial work of his son—Jesus Christ. Jesus secured the exodus of his people who were formerly captives to sin. He did this through the cross.

But the exodus event was not only significant in foreshadowing Christ's work on the cross and the liberation of his people from sin; it also served as a paradigm of hope for the Old Testament saints who were struggling during the time of the Babylonian captivity. This connection is particularly stressed in the prophecies of the prophet Isaiah (Isa. 35:5–10; 40:3–5; 43:14–20; see also Hos. 2:14–16).

The exodus event serves as the most powerful type showing forth the pattern of God's redemption. It is woven through the entire tapestry of Scripture and is

y evident in the very life and work of Jesus
. Just consider the first four chapters of the Gospel
. Matthew, which recount the early life of Jesus and the
beginning of his public ministry. Jesus, like Israel, must
go down to Egypt for a period of time to escape the death
threats of a tyrannical dictator seeking to kill the sons
of Israel (Matt. 2:13–15). In Matthew 2:15, we learn that
Jesus' journey to Egypt and his return therefrom are in
fulfillment of the prophecy of Hosea 11:1, "Out of Egypt
I have called my son." The next major event recorded by
Matthew after Jesus' return from Egypt is his baptism by
John the Baptist in the Jordan River (Matt. 3:13–17). This
parallels the journey of Israel through the waters of the
Red Sea after the exodus from Egypt. Later, like Israel,
Jesus enters the wilderness to encounter the temptation
of Satan, but unlike unfaithful Israel, Jesus overcomes
this temptation by standing firmly upon the Word of
God (Matt. 4:1–11). Of course, the Scriptures that Jesus
uses in his confrontation with Satan all come from the
book of Deuteronomy, which deals with the wilderness
experience of Israel. After this victory over Satan, Jesus
proceeds to give his Sermon on the Mount (Luke 6:17),
in which he proclaims the ethics and imperatives of the
kingdom of God. The parallel here is to Moses' descent
from Mount Sinai with the law of God. The entirety of
Christ's life and work is mirrored in the exodus. The
apostle Paul goes so far as to refer to Jesus as "our Passover lamb" (1 Cor. 5:7).

FROM SERVANT TO SON:
A PROPHET LIKE UNTO MOSES

Clearly, given the significance of the exodus event and
its foreshadowing of the work of Jesus Christ, the book
of Exodus is not ultimately about Moses, but rather about
Jesus. Though the two mediators are inextricably con-

nected, there is no doubt that Jesus eclipses Moses in every regard.

The book of Deuteronomy promised that there would be another like Moses: "The LORD your God will raise up for you a prophet like me from among you, from your fellow Israelites. You must listen to him" (Deut. 18:15). The New Testament confirms that this prophet like Moses is Jesus Christ. For instance, note the allusion to the end of Deuteronomy 18:15 (the command to listen to Moses) in Matthew 17:5, which records the words of the Father when Jesus ascended the Mount of Transfiguration: "While he was still speaking, a bright cloud covered them, and a voice from the cloud said, 'This is my Son, whom I love; with him I am well pleased. *Listen to him!*'" (Matt. 17:5). Peter also made a connection between the prophecy of Deuteronomy 18:5 and Jesus in his sermon on the Day of Pentecost:

> Repent, then, and turn to God, so that your sins may be wiped out, that times of refreshing may come from the Lord, and that he may send the Messiah, who has been appointed for you—even Jesus. Heaven must receive him until the time comes for God to restore everything, as he promised long ago through his holy prophets. For Moses said, "The Lord your God will raise up for you a prophet like me from among your own people; you must listen to everything he tells you. Anyone who does not listen to him will be completely cut off from their people." (Acts 3:19–23)

Jesus fulfills and surpasses the work of Moses. As John puts it in his Gospel, "For the law was given through Moses; grace and truth came through Jesus Christ" (John 1:17).

The writer to the Hebrews perhaps makes the clearest exposition of the similarities and differences between Moses and Jesus. In chapter three of that epistle, the writer properly acknowledges the faithfulness of Moses by stating s was "faithful in all God's house" (Heb. 3:2). ᴅeserves credit for his amazing role in redemptive ᴏry and his example of faithfulness to God. But the writer goes on to state that Jesus is worthy "of greater honor than Moses" (Heb. 3:3). What is the primary difference between these two mediators in the mind of the writer to the Hebrews? What is it that affords Jesus greater honor than Moses? The writer makes the distinction clear in Hebrews 3:4–6:

> For every house is built by someone, but God is the builder of everything. "Moses was faithful as a servant in all God's house," bearing witness to what would be spoken by God in the future. But Christ is faithful as the Son over God's house. And we are his house, if indeed we hold firmly to our confidence and the hope in which we glory.

The primary difference between Moses and Jesus is that Moses was God's servant and Jesus is God's Son. Moses at his best could only participate in and foreshadow redemption, but Jesus actually accomplished it for his people. Jesus, as the God-Man, served as the mediator of the covenant of grace which secured, not the deliverance of an ancient nation from the clutches of a ruthless dictator, but rather the salvation of his people from their own sins and the wrath of a holy God. Exodus may be primarily about Moses, but it will utterly fail in its purposes if the life of Moses and the experiences of ancient Israel do not lead you to see the One who is like unto Moses!

FOR FURTHER REFLECTION

1. The introduction argues that Moses is perhaps the most significant figure of the Old Testament given his unique role as mediator of the old cov-

enant. Review the following references to Moses
in the New Testament and discuss how they reveal
Moses' significance in redemptive history: Matthew 17:3–4; John 1:17; Luke 24:44; Acts 3:19–23;
Hebrews 11:24–29.

2. Read Genesis 12:1–3, 5, 17 and consider how this
   text relates to the story of the book of Exodus.

3. Discuss how the exodus event of the Old Testament
   foreshadows the person and work of Jesus Christ,
   particularly in regard to his redemptive work.

4. Read Hebrews 3:2–6. List the parallels between
   Jesus and Moses. Also consider how Jesus' ministry surpassed and eclipsed the ministry of Moses.

CHAPTER ONE

THE POWER OF
PROVIDENCE

Exodus 1:1–2:10

M y wife and I once attended a play entitled *All in the Timing*, by David Ives. The play is made up of six short comedic sketches, one of which is called "The Philadelphia." In this sketch, one character enters the scene complaining about his day. He declares that everything is going wrong for him. When he explains his predicament to a friend, the friend tells him that he is experiencing these problems because he is in a "Philadelphia." The friend used the phrase "in a Philadelphia" to describe a day in which everything you try to accomplish is thwarted. That phrase stuck with us, and, while we have nothing against the city of Philadelphia (it is a wonderful place!), my wife and I sometimes employ this phrase to describe one of those days in our lives when it seems like nothing is going our way. We just look at each other and say, "I am in a Philadelphia."

Have you ever been "in a Philadelphia," experiencing one of those days in which everything goes wrong?" Have you ever wondered where God is on days like that? I know that when I am in a "Philadelphia" I am often tempted to ask, "Where are you, God?" Perhaps you do too.

As we commence our journey into the life of Moses, we learn that at the time of his birth the Israelites were in a "Philadelphia" of sorts (or perhaps it would be better to say they were in an "Egypt"!). Everything had gone wrong for them. The glorious promises made to Abraham seemed to have fallen to the ground. It must have seemed to them that all hope was lost. But God never forgets his promises, his people, or his plan. In his marvelous providence, we know that "in all things God works for the good of those who love him" (Rom. 8:28)—even when we are in a "Philadelphia." Israel would eventually realize this, but in the opening chapters of Exodus they must have been doubtful about this reality. Just as we often do during difficult times, Israel was likely questioning the power of God's providence to work all things together for their good. But it was at the moment when all must have seemed lost to Israel that God sent forth his redeemer and thus revealed the glorious power of his providence.

FROM PROMISE TO PERIL

For us to understand properly the mindset of the Israelites prior to Moses' birth, we must first consider who they were before everything went wrong. It is important to remember that when Israel entered Egypt four hundred years earlier, the people were filled with promise and hope regarding the future. There were two reasons why the Israelites had such great hope when they first entered Egypt.

First, the Israelites were God's chosen people. They were the descendants of Abraham and thus heirs to the covenant promises made to him in Genesis 12, 15, and 17. As children of Abraham, the Israelites were promised that they would be prosperous (Gen. 17:6), that they would produce a lineage of kings (Gen. 17:6), and that they would inherit the entire land of Canaan. In addition, God promised that his covenant would be "everlasting"; it would extend for generations (Gen. 17:7).

The second reason they were filled with hope upon entering Egypt was the fact that it was God himself who had told them to go there. God visited Jacob in a night vision and told him to take his family to Egypt (Gen. 46:1–4). At that time, the children of Israel were experiencing a great famine and there was food in Egypt. Further, not only was there food, but God had also placed his servant Joseph there and had raised him to a position of power in Pharaoh's court. Even more than that, God promised to be with his people while they were in Egypt and he promised to prosper them:

> "I am God, the God of your father," he said. "Do not be afraid to go down to Egypt, for I will make you into a great nation there. I will go down to Egypt with you, and I will surely bring you back again. And Joseph's own hand will close your eyes. (Gen. 46:3–4)

God promised Israel (as Jacob and his descendants would henceforth be known) that he had nothing to fear about going to Egypt. God promised to be with his people, to prosper them, and to bring them back.

When Israel first arrived in Egypt, they witnessed the fulfillment of God's promises and became a great nation there (Ex. 1:7). At this point, the Israelites had everything going for them. They had survived the famine and had prospered in Egypt just as God had promised. The Egyptians did not like Israel's prosperity and made efforts to suppress them, but the Israelites continually rose to the top. Everything was going their way, but that was about to change. Israel was about to enter a "Philadelphia," and it began with these words: "Then a new king, to whom Joseph meant nothing, came to power in Egypt" (Ex. 1:8).

FROM BAD TO WORSE

When the new Pharaoh came to power everything changed; everything began to go wrong for Israel. The once prosperous and powerful Israelites soon found themselves as lowly slaves. The Egyptians came to dread them (Ex. 1:12) and worked the Israelites ruthlessly (Ex. 1:13); they "made their lives bitter with harsh labor" (Ex. 1:14). The Israelites were now in bondage to a foreign nation.

In addition to facing ruthless treatment and slavery, the Israelites faced another, even more horrifying, threat—the slaughter of their sons. Although the Egyptians had made their lives bitter, the Israelites were still multiplying in number, much to the alarm of Pharaoh, who feared that they would become a military rival. So Pharaoh hatched an evil plan to control the population growth:

> The king of Egypt said to the Hebrew midwives, whose names were Shiphrah and Puah, "When you are helping the Hebrew women during childbirth on the delivery stool, if you see that the baby is a boy, kill him; but if it is a girl, let her live." (Ex. 1:15–16)

Pharaoh ordered the Hebrew midwives to kill every Israelite baby boy. The Hebrew midwives, however, courageously obstructed Pharaoh's plan. They remained faithful to God and refused to implement the plan. This frustrated Pharaoh and led him to employ a more direct strategy for the elimination of Hebrew boys. "Then Pharaoh gave this order to all his people: 'Every Hebrew boy that is born you must throw into the Nile, but let every girl live'" (Ex. 1:22).

As you can see, everything was going wrong for Israel. They had come to Egypt filled with confidence and assurance of God's promises, but soon found themselves in harsh slavery and under the ruthless oversight of their Egyptian taskmasters. Even worse than that, a Pharaoh who was unfamiliar with Joseph had mustered his entire nation against them. The Nile was about to become the graveyard of Israel's future. Just pause and consider what Israel's mindset must have been at this moment. The people must have felt like they were in a "Philadelphia." The children of promise were now slaves to a foreign king. They must have been asking questions like, "Where are you, God?" and "Why is this happening to us?"

WHERE ARE YOU, GOD?

Although few of us have faced the type of persecution that the Israelites faced in Egypt, we do sometimes find ourselves in difficult and challenging circumstances which lead us to ask the questions, "Where are you, God?" and "Why is this happening to me?" As Christians, we all give verbal assent to the truth of Romans 8:28, that God "in all things works for the good of those who love him," but it is much easier to assent to this truth when things are going our way. When hard providences crash upon the shores of our lives in seemingly relentless waves, the truth of Romans 8:28 is easy to question and doubt. I confess that in the midst of my own personal trials I have had my doubts. How about you? In the midst of your own personal trials have you ever wondered, "What good could possibly come out of this?"

While it can be difficult to trust God in challenging circumstances, it is often when things seem most perilous that he works most powerfully. God often sows the seeds of redemption in the seemingly barren soil of despair. God enjoys confounding the conventional wisdom of our world, and he often does this by snatching victory out of the jaws of defeat. We can see an example of this in how God delivered Israel from their predicament in Egypt.

THE POWER OF GOD'S PROVIDENCE

If there had been a twenty-four-hour news network like CNN in the days before Moses' birth, the headlines that would have been flashing across the screen might have been something like this: "Hebrews Continue in Slavery; No End in Sight," "Hebrew Sons to Be Tossed in the Nile," and "God's Promises: Fact or Fiction?" In other words, things were very bleak for the Hebrews and they knew it. But even at this bleak moment, the hand of God's providence was at work planting the seeds of a plan that would eventually blossom into the redemption of his people and the fulfillment of his promises to them.

God's plan required a leader and mediator through whom God would bring about his deliverance. God's purpose required a human vessel and that vessel was Moses. But Moses was about to enter the world at what seemed like the worst possible time; he was born as a Hebrew son at a time when Hebrew sons were doomed to die in the Nile. The plan of God seemed surely destined to fail, but then God intervened in his providence and extracted a glorious victory. From the river of death, God brought life and deliverance.

The power of God's providence can be witnessed in Moses' early life through the amazing way in which he was preserved in the face of Pharaoh's evil edict. Pharaoh had decreed that every Hebrew son must die, but God decreed that he would send a son of the Hebrews to redeem his people. God won. The kings of earth often shake their fists at heaven and declare themselves to be gods, but their decrees and plans have consistently been relegated to the dust heap of history by the power of God's providence. We see this proven once again in Moses' victorious birth.

But the glory of God's providence in the birth of Moses is not seen primarily in the reality that God won, but in how he orchestrated the events that preserved Moses' life in the face of Pharaoh's decree. God plucked the strings of history like a masterful musician. He saved Israel by his providential control over the actions of three women.

THREE WOMEN AND A BABY

The first woman whom God employed in his providential preservation of Moses' life was Moses' mother. God gave Moses a faithful and courageous mother. The most powerful man in Egypt had decreed that all Hebrew sons must die, but when Moses was born his mother subverted Pharaoh's decree, putting herself at personal risk. After his birth, Moses' mother realized there was something special about this child and she hid him from the authorities for three months (Ex. 2:2).

But, eventually, Moses grew too big to be hidden, and so his mother came up with the following plan:

> But when she could hide him no longer, she got a papyrus basket for him and coated it with tar and pitch. Then she placed the child in it and put it among the reeds along the bank of the Nile. (Ex. 2:3)

At first glance, this plan did not seem like a very effective one. After all, the most likely outcome of such a plan was that Moses would die from dehydration, malnutrition, or drowning. Moses' mother was seemingly leaving his survival to chance. It may have been the case that Moses' mother was uncertain of his destiny when she placed him in the water, but it also possible that she knew the location where Pharaoh's daughter came to bathe and strategically placed him in the water so that he would be found by her. Either way, the hand of God's providence was at work in preserving the life of Moses. God was watching over the redeemer of his people.

Exodus 2:4 tells us about the second woman involved in preserving Moses' life: "His sister stood at a distance to see what would happen to him." As his sister was standing there, she noticed that other people were approaching, among them Pharaoh's daughter who was coming to the Nile to bathe. Pharaoh's daughter was to become the third woman God used to preserve Moses' life.

When Pharaoh's daughter arrived, she saw Moses and sent her servant to recover him from the water (Ex. 2:5). As soon as Pharaoh's daughter looked at Moses, she felt "sorry for him," recognizing that Moses was one of the Hebrew babies (Ex. 2:6). She decided to adopt him. This is when Moses' sister jumped into the situation and made the following suggestion to Pharaoh's daughter: "Shall I go and get one of the Hebrew women to nurse the baby for you?" (Ex. 2:7). And whom do you think she fetched to nurse Moses? Of course, she chose Moses' own biological mother!

THE CHAIN OF PROVIDENCE

Just consider the chain of extraordinary providences that preserved Moses' life. His mother hid him for three months. When she could no longer hide him she put him in a basket among the reeds of the Nile on the exact day and time, and at the exact location, that Pharaoh's daughter was coming to bathe. Moses' sister just happened to be watching all of this and just happened to think of a great plan to suggest a Hebrew wet nurse. On top of all this, Pharaoh's daughter, in direct rebellion to her father's decree, felt pity on Moses and adopted him into the most powerful house in Egypt. Moses was supposed to be dead, but instead he grew up in the house of the leader whom, through God's power, he would one day bring to ruin.

When we behold the chain of providential events that God used to preserve Moses' life, we learn a bit about God's *modus operandi*. *Modus operandi* is simply a fancy Latin way of describing how someone likes to operate, a pattern of acting. God has a redemptive *modus operandi*. One aspect of God's redemptive *modus operandi* shines forth in his preservation of Moses—irony. Simply stated, God loves irony. Just consider the ironies present in the chain of events that led to Moses' preservation.

First, the Nile was a place where Israel's hope was to be extinguished, for the river was to be the place where its sons would die. But God brought forth from that supposed graveyard the life of his son and servant Moses, whom he would eventually employ in the redemption of his people. Second, consider the fact that it was from Pharaoh's house that the edict went forth to kill the sons of the Hebrews, but through God's providence, it was from Pharaoh's own house, by means of his daughter's compassion, that Moses was saved from that very edict. Finally, consider the irony of the weak defeating the strong. Moses comes into the world as a little defenseless baby and is saved by three women. In contrast, Pharaoh was the most powerful man in the world. Yet, these three women and a baby sowed the seeds of Pharaoh's demise.

Through this amazing and ironic chain of providential events, God preserved the life of Moses and set in motion the wheels of his unfolding plan of redemption. Moses was exactly where he needed to be to serve in his role as mediator. He would be raised with the knowledge of his Hebrew identity (because of his mother's presence), while simultaneously being raised in all of the wisdom and knowledge of Egypt. God had indeed worked all things together for good for his people!

THE POWER OF PROVIDENCE IN OUR LIVES

While the events of our lives may seem incredibly trivial in comparison to the major events that have unfolded in God's redemptive plan, this divine pattern of God bringing good things out of bad is replicated in the pattern of our lives. The truth of Romans 8:28 is, in fact, most relevant and true at those very moments when we are most likely to place its truth in doubt. God always "works all things together for the good of those who love him" (Rom. 8:28). Our problem is that we often do not see or understand his gentle hand of providence while we are in the midst of trouble. Yet, even in our most desperate moments, he is there. He is there working all things together for good for us.

While we always need to exercise care when drawing parallels between the operation of God's providence in our own personal lives and in God's grand redemptive plan, I think Scripture clearly teaches that the power of God's providence is at work in our own lives. This individual aspect of God's providence is affirmed by the simple comforting words of Matthew 10:30, "And even the very hairs of your head are all numbered." God does pay attention to our lives.

The Westminster Larger Catechism echoes this individual aspect of God's providence in its answer to the question "What are God's works of providence?": "God's works of providence are his most holy, wise, and powerful preserving and governing *all his creatures*; ordering them, and *all their actions*, to his own glory" (emphasis mine). Moses wasn't the only person who experienced the power of God's providence; every believer enjoys this privilege.

What this means for us is that when we are in a "Philadelphia" and everything seems to be breaking bad in our lives, we can be comforted by the knowledge that God is aware of our struggles and, more importantly, will use our trials for our good and his glory. But it is important to remember that while we are in our struggles we may not recognize God's providence at work. Providence is something that is often understood at the human experiential level only in retrospect. We usually require some distance to gain enough perspective to see the power and glory of God's providence in our lives.

This need of chronological distance was present in the account of Moses' preservation as well. While we know the end of the story, Moses' mother did not. For example, when she placed him in a basket she had no idea that God would preserve her son, that he would be raised in Pharaoh's house, and that she would be called upon to be his wet nurse. At the existential moment when she placed her son in the basket, she likely thought she would never see him again. Like so many aspects of the Christian life, we are called to exercise faith in regard to God's providence. This is true even when our story does not end well and things do not turn out "right" in the end. Even when we fail to experience a "happy ending," God is still working for our good and displaying his glory. Admittedly, it requires great faith to trust in God when we suffer difficult providences, but we do not exercise that faith in a void. We have a greater assurance of the truth of Romans 8:28 because we have seen how God, through his providence, orchestrated our deliverance from bondage to sin through the One who is greater than Moses.

THE ONE GREATER THAN MOSES

While the account of God's preserving and protecting of Moses does provide us with comfort regarding the power of God's providence in our lives, its most important function is to point us forward to the work of Jesus Christ. Like Moses, Jesus was born at a time when Israel was under the foot of a foreign power. In Moses' time it was the Egyptians and in Jesus' time it was the Romans. Again, as with Moses, Jesus was born when a powerful leader, King Herod, issued a decree to slaughter Israelite male children. Of course, like Moses, Jesus was preserved from this decree by the providence of God and the faithful actions of his parents.

But while there are many comparisons that can be drawn between the life of Moses and that of Jesus, there are also great contrasts to be made. One of the most important contrasts is in regard to the scope of redemption provided by the two mediators. Moses matured to become the mediator of the old covenant and the human vessel through whom God delivered his people out of their bondage to the Egyptians. But, in stark contrast, Jesus was the mediator of a new and more glorious covenant; he personally delivered his people and he delivered and saved them from sin, death, and the wrath of God. Jesus' work of redemption was clearly greater than that of Moses. This is why the writer of the Epistle to the Hebrews reminds his congregation, and by implication us, how important it is for us to fix our eyes on Jesus and to recognize that he far surpasses the glory of Moses:

> Therefore, holy brothers and sisters, who share in the heavenly calling, fix your thoughts on Jesus, whom we acknowledge as our apostle and high priest. He was faithful to the one who appointed him, just as Moses was faithful in all God's house. Jesus has been found worthy of greater honor than Moses, just as the builder of a house has greater honor than the house itself. For every house is built by someone, but God is the builder of everything. "Moses was faithful as a servant in all God's house," bearing witness to what would be spoken by God in the future. But Christ is faithful as the Son over God's house. And we are his house, if indeed we hold firmly to our confidence and the hope in which we glory. (Heb. 3:11–6)

Yes, Moses was a faithful servant in God's house, but Jesus is God's faithful Son. His glory far surpasses Moses' and the glory of the exodus is eclipsed by the glory of God's providence in bringing about our redemption through Jesus.

All of Jesus' glorious redemptive work was part of a plan forged by the Father before the foundation of the world and perfectly orchestrated in time. As Galatians 4:4–5 reminds us, Jesus came into this world according to the exact timing of God's providence: "But when the set time had fully come, God sent his Son, born of a woman, born under the law, to redeem those under the law, that we might receive adoption to sonship." Jesus came into the world according to God's providential plan and God once again worked the glories of his redemptive irony in a manner that confounded the world and reaffirmed the reality of Romans 8:28. He did this by securing our victory at the moment of seeming defeat. Just think about Jesus on the cross. There was the self-proclaimed Son of God hanging from a cross and seemingly subject to the Roman Empire and its decrees. To his disciples this seemed like the bleakest moment in human history—the Savior of the World was crucified at the hands of men. Yet, in the greatest irony of all, it was at that very moment of seeming defeat that the greatest victory in history was won by the power of God. Jesus rose from the dead victorious and in doing so proved to the utmost the reality of these words: "And we know in all things God works for the good of those who love him."

FOR FURTHER REFLECTION

1. It is very challenging to trust God during difficult times. As we saw in this chapter, Israel faced this challenge during their time of bondage in Egypt. Can you think of a time in your life when you had to trust God during a difficult time? How did you cope? What did you learn from this experience?

2. God commenced his plan of delivering Israel from bondage in Egypt at the very time when all hope seemed lost. Can you think of other times in

redemptive history when God delivered his people at a time when all seemed lost? How is this pattern manifested in the work of Jesus?

3. Moses almost perished as a child, but was saved through a chain of providentially orchestrated events. Can you look back on your life and see a similar chain of providence in how God delivered you from a trial?

4. Read Galatians 6:4–5. This text speaks about the providential coming of Jesus Christ in history at the exact time appointed by God. In John's Gospel, Jesus frequently refers to his "hour" (John 2:4; 4:21, 23; 5:25, 28; 7:6, 8, 30; 8:20; 12:23; 12:27). How do the "hour" texts of John's Gospel relate to Galatians 6:4–5 and what do these texts reveal about God's role in history and redemption?

CHAPTER TWO

ONE OF LIFE'S DETOURS

Exodus 2:11–25

Have you ever been driving and come upon a sign that reads, "Detour?" I hate it when that happens. I find detours extremely frustrating. They take you on unfamiliar roads, in a direction that you did not plan to go, and delay your arrival at your destination. Detours always result in wasted time.

Detours occur not only on the highways, but also sometimes in our lives. Sometimes we are planning on heading in one direction in life, then circumstances change drastically, sending us in a totally unexpected direction. Have you ever experienced a detour like this in your own life? I have experienced these detours many times.

Sometimes my detours came as a result of circumstances beyond my control. Perhaps this has happened to you. Detours are sometimes the result of unforeseen events related to our health, employment, or family situation. At other times, however, I have caused my detours through my own deliberate actions and decisions. Sometimes these detours have been a product of wise and godly decisions, but I have also created detours in my life through unwise and rash decisions. Regardless of the cause of my life detours, when I encounter them my first reaction is very similar to the reaction I have when coming upon a detour while travelling in my car—I feel like I am wasting time in reaching my ultimate destination.

When Moses was around forty years old, he too experienced one of life's detours. The course of his life was altered by an unwise and rash decision. This detour in Moses' life was significant; it lasted forty years. My guess is that during that lengthy detour Moses must have felt like that part of his life was an incredible waste of time. But actually God used this detour to prepare Moses for his role as mediator of the old covenant.

A MAN OF PRIVILEGE

If we are to understand how God used the detour in Moses' life to prepare him for his calling, we must first understand what caused the detour and why it was necessary for Moses to have such a course correction. The root cause was pride—pride crept into Moses' heart because of his privileged background. During the first forty years of Moses' life he was a man with many advantages.

As we saw in the previous chapter, the first privilege that Moses enjoyed was God's providential care. When Moses had no capacity to defend himself, God orchestrated his steps, and the steps of others, to ensure Moses' survival. As a young man, Moses also enjoyed the privileges of royalty. He was raised as a prince in Egypt. Because of this he never went without anything. Unlike his fellow Israelites, Moses never lived as a servant; rather, others served him. A third privilege Moses enjoyed in his youth was a first-class education. Moses received religious instruction from his mother, so he understood the wisdom of God, but he also received a top-notch secular education in Egypt: "Moses was educated in all the wisdom of the Egyptians and was powerful in speech and action" (Acts 7:22). Moses had the privilege of learning both godly and worldly knowledge.

Finally, Moses was blessed with the privilege of a divine calling. He was called to be the mediator of the old covenant and the deliverer of God's people. Even though Moses was not yet aware of the full scope of this calling during his youth, the Scriptures reveal that he had some sense of this role. We know this because when he observed an Egyptian beating a Hebrew, Moses described the Hebrew as "one of his own people" (Ex. 2:11). Stephen's sermon, particularly Acts 7:24–26, confirms the idea that Moses had a sense that God had called him to rescue his people. Moses had the privilege of being called by God to a great task.

Moses was clearly a privileged man, but like many men of privilege he allowed this privilege to give birth to personal pride and self-sufficiency. It was his pride that would bring about his fall and his forty-year detour.

A MAN OF PRIDE

Privilege often leads to pride. We hear stories like this every day in our world. Young men and women, who grow up surrounded by wealth and opportunity, allow their privilege to lead to personal pride. Often these stories do not end well as these young people perceive themselves as operating above the law and according to their own standards. This usually leads to their destruction and the loss of their advantages. When the seeds of privilege yield the harvest of pride, God sends correction; he did this in the life of Moses by sending him on a detour.

The detour in Moses' life was caused by his prideful act that is recorded in Exodus 2:11–14. In this account we learn that Moses observed a Hebrew man being beaten by an Egyptian and he responded by killing the Egyptian. At first glance, Moses' actions, while wrong, seem to be motivated by sympathy for his fellow Hebrew and caused by impulsive, "heat of the moment" decision making. Also, other passages of Scripture, at least at first glance, seem to vindicate Moses for this rash decision. But when we examine more closely what occurred here, we see that Moses' decision was wrong and was motivated by his own prideful self-sufficiency. There are two ways in which we see Moses' pride in his decision to kill the Egyptian.

First, we see his pride in the fact that he attempted to impose his own timetable for the deliverance of the Hebrews. Moses understood that one of his own was being harmed here, and he also had some sense of his calling to be involved in the liberation of his people, but God had not yet revealed the plan for this deliverance. Accordingly, when Moses inserted himself into this situation, he was presuming that he understood his role and that it operated according to his own timetable. Whenever we attempt to replace God's timetable with our own, we are acting in a prideful manner.

A second way in which Moses' pride emerges in this account is the method that Moses chose to employ in the liberation of his people. God had a plan for how he would deliver the Israelites, a plan constructed to display God's glory and power. Moses' plan involved using his own physical strength. God's plan of deliverance was intended to publicly display his glory, but Moses' method involved an act in secret to hide his shame. We can see Moses' shame in the fact that he looked to the left and the right to make sure no one saw his deeds (Ex. 2:12). Whenever we substitute our methods for God's methods we are acting in a prideful manner.

These prideful actions of Moses—using his own timetable and employing his own methods—are things we struggle with all the time as Christians. It is so easy for us to convince ourselves that God is not moving fast enough or that his methods are inefficient. I often face the temptation to accomplish my goals in my timing and in my way. Perhaps you too struggle with this temptation. The reality is that when we engage in this type of prideful behavior we are essentially declaring that we believe we are sovereign over our own lives and circumstances. Autonomy, pride, and self-sufficiency are simply a reflection of our self-love and self-idolatry. The end result of this type of pride is set forth for us in Proverbs 16:18, which says, "Pride goes before destruction, a haughty spirit before a fall." This is exactly what happened to Moses after his prideful actions—he experienced a destructive fall.

The first destructive consequence of Moses' prideful actions was that they led him to being discredited among his own people. We can see this reality in the response that he received when he tried to break up an altercation between two Hebrews on the day after he killed the Egyptian. One of the Hebrew men in the fight said to Moses, "'Who made you ruler and judge over us? Are you thinking of killing me as you killed the Egyptian?' Then Moses was afraid and thought, 'What I did must have become known'" (Ex. 2:14). Because of his pride, Moses had lost his moral authority as a leader of his own people.

Moses' pride also made him an enemy of Pharaoh. When Pharaoh learned of Moses' actions, he became angry and sought to kill Moses (Ex. 2:15). Moses was discredited among his own people and the Egyptians. He was a man without a people and without a country. He became a fugitive from the law and had only one choice—to run.

By his prideful actions, Moses was implying that he could go it alone. By using his own timetable and methods, Moses was declaring that he did not need God. The result of his prideful attitude and actions was that God let him go it alone for a while. Moses ran off alone to Midian. He ventured onto a great detour that would delay his involvement in the deliverance of God's people for forty years. But this forty-year detour was not wasted time; rather, it was necessary because Moses was not yet ready for service. He needed more preparation and that's exactly how God used this detour in Moses' life.

A MAN PREPARED

Moses' pride led him on a detour to nowhere. He found himself in the desert land of Midian. There he was a foreigner, a failure, and a fugitive. Gone were the pomp, circumstance, and luxuries of Pharaoh's house. Whereas he had once been a son in Pharaoh's palace, now he was reduced to being a lowly shepherd in the desert (Ex. 3:1). Once he had prospects of being the deliverer of the Hebrew people, but now he was a captive himself.

Moses must have thought that all was lost, but in actuality it was his forty years in the desert that prepared him to be what he was destined to become—God's servant to deliver the Israelites out of bondage. Before he experienced this detour, Moses lacked two essential qualities that God requires of his servants: empathy and humility. Moses would cultivate both of these fruitful attributes while in the barren desert of Midian.

We know that Moses had a sense of connection with the Hebrew people prior to his detour to Midian. But while Moses had a sense that he was a Hebrew and ethnically identified with them, prior to his detour he lacked any real sense of what it was like to *be* a Hebrew in Egypt. Remember, Moses was a Hebrew who grew up in Pharaoh's house. He knew nothing of the slavery and suffering of his people. But then in Midian he found himself in a form of bondage. He had been taken from his land and placed in a strange land among a strange people. He had lost his privileges. He had to work for a living, and he became a shepherd. In Midian he got a taste of what it was like to be a Hebrew in slavery in a foreign land. He could now identify and empathize with the Hebrew people whom he was destined to deliver by the power of God.

Empathy is one of the qualities God demands from those called to be his servants. A deliverer in God's kingdom is required to identify and relate to those he is delivering. Moses began to understand the condition of the

Hebrews while in Midian. He was now truly one of them and was prepared to lead and deliver them. Scripture attests to the development of this empathy in Moses in the words that the writer to the Hebrews uses to describe Moses in Hebrews 11:24–26:

> By faith Moses, when he had grown up, refused to be known as the son of Pharaoh's daughter. He chose to be mistreated along with the people of God rather than to enjoy the fleeting pleasures of sin. He regarded disgrace for the sake of Christ as of greater value than the treasures of Egypt, because he was looking ahead to his reward.

Moses "chose to be mistreated along with the people of God." When he saw the Hebrew being beaten by the Egyptian he had a sense of ethnic identity, but in Midian he began to embody a sense of ethnic empathy. It was in the desert of Midian that Moses truly learned what it was like to be a Hebrew.

Moses also learned humility while in Midian. Before Midian, Moses was full of himself. In Midian, he learned to be empty of self. It would be very easy to become full of yourself if you were raised in a setting of privilege like Moses was. You would never experience want, you would have servants at your beck and call, and everyone would cater to you and your needs.

While our culture sometimes admires and advances people who are full of themselves, God operates a very different type of economy. God requires his appointed leaders to empty themselves of pride and privilege. God seeks a humble and contrite heart and hates a prideful heart. God calls us to empty ourselves of ourselves. Interestingly, Moses began to understand this principal of emptiness at a place of filling.

After fleeing Egypt, Moses found himself near a well where seven daughters of a Midianite priest had come to fill their troughs (Ex. 2:16–17). But the seven daughters were being harassed by some shepherds and were prevented access to the well. When Moses saw this, he "got up and came to their rescue and watered their flock" (Ex. 2:17). Moses' response reveals a massive change of heart. Think about what he did here. The women he assisted were not Hebrews and yet he helped them, and he did so without violence. He did not violate any commandments in pride and haste. Further, he not only rescued these women, but he also "watered their flock" (Ex. 2:17).

Now think about Moses' actions for a moment. He had just left Egypt, where he was served by others and had never really engaged in any hard labor. Yet, here we find Moses serving a group of foreign women. He took the role of a servant. When he entered Midian, he began to serve rather than be served. He emptied himself of "self" and began to put the interests of others before his own. His fall from grace in Egypt and this episode in Midian put Moses on a path toward humility and service to others. It was a lesson he learned so well that in Numbers 12:3 he is described in these terms: "Now Moses was a very humble man, more humble than anyone else on the face of the earth." It was in the desert of Midian that Moses learned to be a servant; he learned about humility and its importance in God's kingdom. Moses' detour in Midian was not wasted time; it was time redeemed by God to prepare his servant.

PREPARED FOR SERVANTHOOD?

It is worth pausing to note how these two qualities, empathy and humility, are not only prerequisites for leadership in God's kingdom, but are also marks of the mature Christian life. All Christians are called to cultivate empathy and humility. Consider, for example,

the following call for empathy issued by Paul from Philippians 2:2–4:

> Therefore if you have any encouragement from being
> united with Christ, if any comfort from his love, if
> any common sharing in the Spirit, if any tenderness
> and compassion, then make my joy complete by
> being like-minded, having the same love, being one
> in spirit and of one mind. Do nothing out of selfish
> ambition or vain conceit. Rather, in humility value
> others above yourselves, not looking to your own
> interests but each of you to the interests of the others.

Like Moses, we are called to move the focus off of ourselves
and instead consider the lives, circumstances, needs, and
interests of others. We are called to empathy.

How are you doing in this area of your Christian walk?
Are you like Moses before Midian, being consumed with
your selfish ambition and pride? Or have you learned that
the Christian life is about serving rather than being served?
Have you, like Moses, learned how to water the flocks of
others?

Similarly, as Christians we are all called to humility.
Humility involves self-emptying. Jesus makes it quite clear
that the Christian life requires that we first empty ourselves
so that we may find ourselves: "Whoever finds their life
will lose it, and whoever loses their life for my sake will
find it" (Matt. 10:39). It is as if we are like a glass and we
begin by being filled with ourselves. The glass full of self
must be poured out like water, and then, and only then,
can we begin to be filled with Christ. The idea that fullness begins with emptiness is one of the many paradoxes
of the Christian life.

What is in the glass of your life? Are you like Moses
before Midian, filled with self-love and pride, or have you
learned what Moses learned? The fullness of life with God
is found only when we empty our lives of self-love.

A LIFE WITHOUT DETOURS

We have seen that Moses required a detour in his life to equip him with the requisite attributes to become a successful servant-leader in God's kingdom. Moses had to go through Midian before he could lead God's people out of Egypt. His time in Midian was anything but wasted time. His detour, like many of our own detours, was used by God to prepare him for his calling. We, like Moses, often require a course correction in our lives. But Moses' detour not only serves to remind us of how God uses our mistakes to mold us for service; more importantly, it points us to the glory of Jesus.

The people and events of the Old Testament often serve as types in foreshadowing the glory of Jesus and the new covenant. Sometimes these Old Testament types show us Jesus by means of their Christlike actions, but other times they show us the glory of Jesus by means of their failures and inadequacies. The latter is the case here with Moses' detour.

Moses is arguably the most revered Old Testament saint. He is certainly in the top three, along with Abraham and David. But, as with Abraham and David, Moses was a flawed man. He was also a flawed mediator. He did not volunteer to become empathetic, but instead was forced into it by his own sinful actions. Moses also did not willingly humble himself, but instead he had to have the glass of his life poured out forcefully by God sending him to Midian.

In contrast, when we look at the life of our Savior, we see a starkly different picture. Jesus required no detour in his life. He was always singularly focused on the fulfilling of his Father's will. In Jesus, empathy and humility were always there and they were made manifestly evident in his incarnation and work on the cross. Listen to how Paul describes Jesus in Philippians 2:6–8:

Who, being in very nature God, did not consider equality with God something to be used to his own advantage; rather, he made himself nothing by taking the very nature of a servant, being made in human likeness. And being found in appearance as a man, he humbled himself by becoming obedient to death—even death on a cross!

Like Moses, Jesus was sent to deliver his people out of bondage, but Jesus willingly submitted to becoming like us so that he could deliver us. He understood that he had to identify and empathize with the people he came to save:

> For this reason he had to be made like them [or like his brothers], fully human in every way, in order that he might become a merciful and faithful high priest in service to God, and that he might make atonement for the sins of the people. (Heb. 2:17)

He was willing to be born of a woman and born under the law that he himself made in order to "redeem those under the law" and so that we "might receive adoption to sonship" (Gal. 4:4–5).

Unlike Moses, Jesus required no detours and he never deviated from the path of God's will. It is this glorious reality that gives us hope and assurance in our salvation. Our redeemer, unlike Moses, never deviated from the course of his calling, and because of his steadfast, unswerving, and perfect obedience, we are delivered from the bondage of slavery to sin.

FOR FURTHER REFLECTION

1. This chapter focuses on a detour in Moses' life that took him in a direction that he did not want to go, but ultimately made him more useful to God. Have you ever taken such a detour in your life?

2. Moses was raised as a boy of privilege in the house of Pharaoh. Can you name some of these privileges? What impact did these privileges have on Moses' character?

3. Discuss how Moses' prideful attitude manifested itself in his slaying of the Egyptian. Can you think of other biblical passages which address the sin of pride?

4. What were the two big lessons that Moses learned while exiled in Midian? How did these two lessons prepare Moses for leadership? Do you think these lessons are still relevant for believers and church leaders today? If so, why are they important?

5. How does Moses' detour help us to see the greater glory of Jesus Christ?

CHAPTER THREE

A LIFE-CHANGING ENCOUNTER

Exodus 3:1–10

O ne day I was sitting in political science class at college when I took notice of a young woman sitting a few desks away from me. She seemed very intelligent to me and also very attractive. That day in class we were discussing the writings of John Calvin and the operation of the city of Geneva during the time of the Reformation. I was not a Christian at that point and was a bit skeptical of Calvin's worldview. After class I engaged the young woman in a conversation during which she advised me that she actually believed in Calvin's theology and invited me to attend her "Calvinist" church. I took her up on this offer and visited her church. Eventually, by God's grace and the ministry of that church, I came to embrace the gospel of Jesus Christ. I also married that young woman (you probably saw that coming!). That day in political science class changed my life.

Have you ever had a life-changing encounter? Have you ever met someone who ultimately altered the course of your life? I am guessing that you have experienced this on some level. Perhaps, like me, you met the love of your life, or maybe you met someone who profoundly influenced your career choice. Of course, if you are a Christian, then you have certainly had a life-changing encounter because you have met the risen Lord. In fact, the entire Bible is really a story of a life-changing encounter between God and man. God, in his merciful condescension, chose to encounter humanity and entered into a covenant with our first parents. After the fall, God, in his gracious condescension, once again chose to encounter his people through a covenant of grace whereby his people would be redeemed through the work of Jesus Christ.

When we meet God, be it like Paul on the road to Damascus, or through the preached Word, our lives are irrevocably altered. One cannot meet the holy and living God and remain unchanged and unaffected by it. Moses had one of those life-changing encounters with God near Mount Horeb (also known as Mount Sinai) while tending his father-in-law's flocks on the far side of the desert.

As we explore Moses' life-changing encounter, we will examine where it happened, who he encountered, what occurred in that encounter, and why God initiated the encounter. In other words, we will look at the where, who, what, and why of this encounter.

THE MOUNTAINS OF MOSES' LIFE

When we experience a life-changing encounter we often recall vividly where it occurred. For instance, I will never forget the political science classroom in which I met my wife for the first time. In the Bible, the "where" of an encounter with God often carries great significance. That is certainly the case here. God chose to meet Moses at Mount Horeb, the "mountain of God" (Ex. 3:1). Mount Horeb is generally agreed by scholars to be another name for Mount Sinai. God met Moses at a mountain, God's mountain.

If you read the Bible carefully, you will quickly note that mountains play an important role in God's revelation.

It is often the case that crucial redemptive events occur at mountains. For example, in the Old Testament, the garden of Eden is described as a mountain (Ezek. 28:13–15) and Abraham's effort to sacrifice Isaac and God's provision of a sacrifice occurred at a mountain (Gen. 22:1–14). The New Testament continues to exhibit this "mountain motif" as Jesus resisted Satan's temptation on a mountain (Matt. 4:8; Luke 4:5), delivered his great sermon on a mountain (Matt. 5:1; Mark 3:13), pronounced his Great Commission from a mountain (Matt. 28:16), and later, after his death and resurrection, ascended into heaven from the Mount of Olives (Acts 1:10–12). Mountains play a significant role in God's revelation of himself and the unfolding plan of redemption.

As you can see, where things occur in the Bible is very important, particularly when the "where" is a mountain. Moses' life reveals the truth of this principle. In fact, you can trace the peaks and valleys of Moses' life by literally examining his life from the perspective of the various mountains that are part of his story. As we have already seen, he is about to have a life-changing encounter here at Mount Horeb (Ex. 3). As we will see in this chapter, this will be a very positive development in Moses' life. Later in the book of Exodus, Moses will return to this very same mountain to meet with God again and receive the Ten Commandments (Ex. 19–34). This latter encounter on Mount Sinai is not only the most important event in Moses' life, it is also one of the most important events in the entirety of biblical revelation. The peaks of Moses' life were often experienced on the peak of a mountain. But Moses also experienced some valley moments in his life, and these often occurred while at a mountain as well. For example, later in his life he stood on Mount Pisgah and God allowed him to survey the land of promise, but there God told him that he could not enter the land because of his disobedience in the incident of bringing water from the rock (Deut. 34:1–4).

In God's grace, however, Moses' mountain experiences did not end with the low note of Mount Pisgah. The Bible describes one additional mountain experience in Moses' life. In the New Testament, Jesus takes Peter, James, and John up a "high mountain" (Matt. 17:1); on that mountain Jesus was transfigured before them. Jesus' face shone like the sun and his clothes were bright white, as bright as the light (Matt. 17:2). But Jesus was not alone in that glorious moment of his messianic revelation. Jesus had two companions on that occasion—one was Elijah and the other was Moses. Of all of the mountain moments in Moses' life, none compared to the surpassing glory of being in the presence of his Lord Jesus Christ on the Mount of Transfiguration. This is the moment of Moses' greatest glory as he fulfills his calling of pointing to the prophet and mediator who is greater than he. While Moses may not have entered the dusty ground of the earthly land of promise, there is no doubt that he made it to the Promised Land of heavenly Jerusalem!

The great trek of the mountains of Moses' life began at Mount Horeb. It is at this location where Moses' ministry begins. It is at this mountain that Moses' life changes in profound ways. Ultimately, however, it is not the "where" of this encounter that changes his life and alters his course, but rather the "who" he meets there.

THE ANGEL OF THE LORD

The life-changing encounters of our lives generally involve a dynamic person. Sometimes that person is a teacher, the coach of a team, or a youth group leader. The most important "person" a Christian can encounter, however, is the living God. To be a Christian means that God has intruded into your life, on his own initiative, and changed your life by his wondrous love and grace. In this sense, we share something in common with Moses. For like all Christians, Moses had a life-changing encounter with the living God while at Mount Horeb. But Moses' encounter with God was also quite different from our personal experience of encountering God. What Moses experienced at Mount Horeb was a unique, one-time event in redemptive history in which he physically encountered the angel of the Lord: "There the angel of the LORD appeared to him in flames of fire from within a bush. Moses saw that though the bush was on fire it did not burn up" (Ex. 3:2).

Who was this angel of the Lord? Who met with Moses that day? Was this encounter similar to that of Zechariah in the New Testament where an angel of the Lord visited Zechariah to declare the forthcoming birth of John the Baptist (Luke 1:11–20)? It is unmistakable from the text that Moses did not meet with an intermediary sent from God that day at Mount Horeb, but rather with God himself. We can tell this because it is God's voice that speaks to Moses from the burning bush: "When the LORD saw that he had gone over to look, *God called to him* from within the bush, 'Moses! Moses!'" (Ex. 3:4). In addition to the presence of God's voice, the text also reveals that this voice clearly identifies who he is:

> "Do not come any closer," God said. "Take off your sandals, for the place where you are standing is holy ground." Then he said, "I am the God of your father, the God of Abraham, the God of Isaac and the God of Jacob." At this, Moses hid his face, because he was afraid to look at God.

The one whose voice cried out from the bush declared himself to be God. Moses did not meet with a mere angel that day, which would have been extraordinary in its own right; instead, Moses experienced something even more extraordinary that day: he experienced a direct personal encounter with the Great I Am. This conclusion finds further support in the fact that Moses is instructed to take off his sandals because he is standing on "holy ground" (Ex. 3:4).

Most scholars agree that what Moses experienced that day was a theophany—a visible manifestation of God. Some even contend that Moses encountered the preincarnate Son of God in the burning bush. While it is not exegetically settled that this represents an encounter with the Son of God, it is abundantly clear that Moses encountered the living and powerful God who manifested his presence to his servant by means of a burning bush and the angel of the Lord.

The "who" of this life-changing encounter was the Lord Almighty. God intruded into Moses' life at Mount Horeb. As is always the case with such manifestations of God's power and presence, there was a distinct purpose behind this miraculous display of his glory. God had a mission and mandate for Moses. This brings us to the "what" of this encounter.

THE MISSION OF MOSES

The "what" of Moses' encounter with the Angel of the Lord at Mount Horeb refers to the substance of what was conveyed to Moses there. God called Moses to Mount Horeb because he had a mission for Moses and he communicated it to him in no uncertain terms: "So now, go. I am sending you to Pharaoh to bring my people the Israelites out of Egypt" (Ex. 3:10). It was this calling that would drastically alter the trajectory of Moses' life. Like the World War II posters of Uncle Sam that called young men to enlist in the army, God was pointing his finger at Moses and saying, "I want *you!*"

One might think that Moses' reaction to such an illustrious calling would be to express gratitude to God or to be puffed up with pride. After all, God was choosing Moses from among all of the Israelites to lead God's people out of bondage. God was appointing Moses as the supreme commander over the liberation of the Israelites. What a privilege!

The last time Moses had a sense of this calling it had gone straight to his head, and he usurped God's timetable by killing the Egyptian who was abusing a Hebrew. But Moses was not the same man now. He had his forty years' experience of humbling in the desert of Midian. His first reaction to God's awesome calling upon his life was neither gratitude nor pride; rather, it was doubt and humility: "But Moses said to God, 'Who am I that I should go to Pharaoh and bring the Israelites out of Egypt?'" (Ex. 3:11).

In my opinion, this was one of Moses' best moments and one of his most lucid responses to God. Granted, there were certainly pragmatic reasons for Moses to respond in the manner he did. After all, he was still technically a fugitive from Egypt and had run away from Pharaoh and the Egyptians with his tail between his legs. There was also the reality that he had not seen his Hebrew brethren in forty years and many would likely not even recognize him; those who did would likely recall his shameful exit. In addition to these practical concerns was the reality that Moses was being called to oppose Pharaoh, who was the leader of the mightiest nation in Moses' world. But while there were certainly numerous pragmatic reasons for Moses to want to shrink from this calling, I think there was something more at work here. I think Moses' reaction reflected his humbling and his awareness of his own weaknesses. He was no longer the brash young son of Pharaoh's house. He now understood that attempting to accomplish God's calling in his own power would be a recipe for disaster. Moses never spoke more true words than when he stated, "*Who am I* that I should go to Pharaoh and bring the Israelites out of Egypt?" (Ex. 3:11).

It is often the case that the greatest spiritual strides forward in our lives begin with the question, "Who am I?" The question reflects awareness that without God we can do nothing. This is what Jesus taught when he spoke of the vine and the branches: "I am the vine; you are the branches. If you remain in me and I in you, you will bear much fruit; *apart from me you can do nothing*" (John 15:5). To say "Who am I?" when called to a challenging task does not reflect cowardice or a lack of faith, but rather reflects the knowledge that in our own strength we will fail. Moses now understood his weaknesses and this displayed that he was ready for his calling.

After Moses' self-effacing response to God's amazing calling on his life, God did not accuse Moses of lack of faith, but instead encouraged Moses: "And God said, 'I will be with you. And this will be the sign to you that it is I who have sent you: When you have brought the people out of Egypt, you will worship God on this mountain'" (Ex. 3:12). Note that God encouraged Moses by conveying two things to him—God's presence with him and a sign that assured Moses that his mission would be a success. God filled the void of Moses' self-acknowledged weakness with the fullness of his loving assurance. Moses knew that the Angel of the Lord was with him.

This interchange between God and Moses should provide assurance for all of us. Although we are not called to the unique redemptive-historical mission that God gave to Moses, we all do have a calling from God on our lives. We are all called to be holy and to live for him. This is an insurmountable task in our own strength. There is no way we can be successful in our calling apart from the work of Jesus Christ. Just as with Moses, we must look that calling square in the face and say, "Who am I?" The response we receive from God is very similar to the one that he gave Moses. God's Word tells us that he will be with us (Matt. 28:20; Heb. 13:5) and that he has given us signs to assure us of victory (1 Cor. 11:23–25; Col. 2:11–12). In fact, every time we come to the Lord's Table, or when we are once brought, or come to, the baptismal font, we have that assuring combination of God's presence and a sign confirming our victory through Jesus Christ. Moses had this assurance and it is ours as well through Christ Jesus.

WHY GOD CAME DOWN

Now we come to the last aspect of Moses' life-changing encounter—the "why" of the encounter. Why did God intrude into Moses' life at this particularly significant place, Mount Horeb, and communicate his mission to him through the extraordinary agency of the Angel of the Lord? God makes this clear in Exodus 3:8: "So I have come down to rescue them from the hand of the Egyptians and to bring them up out of that land into a good and spacious land, a land flowing with milk and honey." Why did the "holy one," the consuming fire, reveal himself to a fugitive in the backwaters of Midian? He did it to save his people, to fulfill his promises, and to bring redemption.

The importance of the imagery of God coming "down" to rescue his people should not escape us. This phrase clearly refers to the condescension of God in stooping from his heavenly throne to redeem his earthly people. It not only demonstrates God's love in condescending to redeem those who don't deserve it, but it also reveals the monergistic nature of redemption. Monergism simply means that God is the sole initiator and participant in the work of redemption. He is the active one who makes it possible. This is exactly what happened to Israel during the time of their slavery in Egypt. God determined that the time of their redemption had come and he initiated the process of their redemption by choosing an earthly mediator, Moses, to administer his plan. But the entire process was fuelled by God's condescension, initiative, and redeeming power. All Moses could do is confess in his weakness, "Who am I?"

Of course, the biblical-theological parallels between the imagery of Exodus 3:8 and the work of Jesus Christ are unmistakable. The epitome of God's condescending love is the incarnation of the eternal Son of God. In Jesus Christ, God the Son stooped down and became man. Why did he do this? He did it to redeem his people from bondage to sin and death.

But while there are parallels between the two episodes, the glory of the work of Jesus Christ is also unparalleled in many ways. Israel was freed from bondage to an earthly nation, but Jesus freed us from the much greater foes of sin and death. In reality, Jesus freed us from the wrath of God and made peace between his people and God. Also, in the Exodus account, Moses serves as God's mediator, but in the new covenant it is Jesus, God himself, who serves as the mediator. The work of Jesus completely eclipsed the work that God did through Moses. As John reminds us in his Gospel, "For the law was given through Moses; grace and truth came through Jesus Christ" (John 1:17). Unlike Moses, Jesus would give his perfect life for the redemption of his people. Moses, by the power of God, turned the Nile to blood, but Jesus gave us the sacrifice of his own blood.

This reality of a God who stoops down to save the undeserving is one of the greatest mysteries of our existence, and it speaks to the fathomless depths of God's love. Why did God intrude into the life of Moses? He did it because he loves his people and because his promises will never fall to the ground. He did it because he is the God who redeems his people from bondage.

THE GOD WHO CHANGES PEOPLE

One of the attributes of God is his immutability. When theologians speak of the immutability of God, what they mean, in laymen's terms, is that God does not change. The Bible teaches this truth in many places. For example, consider Malachi 3:6: "I the LORD do not change"; James 1:17: "Every good and perfect gift is from above, coming down from the Father of the heavenly lights, who does not change like shifting shadows"; and Hebrews 13:8: "Jesus Christ is the same yesterday and today and forever." God cannot change and does not change. The reason for this is that he is self-existent, self-sufficient, and perfect. Nothing can act upon him to change him and he has no need to be changed. The same is not true of us. This is why God's immutability is referred to as an "incommunicable" attribute, that is, it is one that is not reflected in or shared by humanity. We are mutable creatures.

While God does not change, thankfully, he intercedes in the lives of his people to change them. Our God changes people. This is good news because we, unlike God, are in need of changing. Because of the fall, all mankind is in an estate of sin and misery and we are subject to God's wrath. The only way out of that horrifying reality is the changeless God who changes people.

Moses understood well this reality in his own life. After messing up his life in his early years, he spent forty long years in a desert. What happened in the dust of Midian? God changed Moses. The culminating event of the changes in Moses' life was the encounter he had with God at Mount Horeb. This was a pivotal point for Moses. He would no longer be a second-rate shepherd in Midian, but he would now become the mediator of the old covenant. Now that's a life-changing encounter!

But Moses wasn't the only biblical figure who had his life changed by an encounter with God. Abram was called by God out of Ur of the Chaldees to become the father of a nation. David, the runt of his family and a mere shepherd boy, was called by God to be the greatest king of the Old Testament, foreshadowing the coming of King Jesus. Peter, James, and John were out fishing one day when Jesus called them to drop their nets and become fishers of men—and they did. Paul was struck blind by Jesus on the road to Damascus and was enlisted to become the apostle to the Gentiles. God has a pattern of intruding into the lives of his creatures to alter who they are.

Now, it is true that none of us have been called to such important roles in God's redemptive plan. The life-changing encounters I have listed are nonrepeatable events. But this does not mean that we have not experienced, or cannot, a life-changing encounter with God. In fact, it occurs quite frequently. It occurs every time a sinner repents and confesses Jesus Christ as Lord. Salvation is a life-changing encounter in which God changes not only the trajectory of our lives, but also who we are. When God stoops down to meet us, through his Word and Spirit and by the work of Jesus Christ, we become new creations: "Therefore, if anyone is in Christ, the new creation has come: The old has gone, the new is here!" (2 Cor. 5:17).

What Moses' life-changing encounter teaches us is that we serve a God who will go to extreme lengths to redeem the lost. He does not cast aside his people because they are unworthy or incapable. Instead he condescends to meet with them, change them, and free them from bondage. The only appropriate response to such glorious grace is, "Who am I?"

FOR FURTHER REFLECTION

1. This chapter focuses on a life-changing encounter that occurred in Moses' life. Have you ever experienced such an encounter in your life?
2. List several significant events in Moses' life that took place at a mountain. Can you think of other significant redemptive-historical events that occurred at a mountain?
3. What is a theophany and how does it relate to the "Angel of the Lord"? Can you think of other theophanies in the Old Testament?
4. How did Moses' response to receiving his mission reveal that he was now ready to assume the role of a servant-leader?

5. Why did God condescend to meet with Moses? What does this tell us about God's role in our salvation?

6. This chapter of Moses' life reveals how God changes people. Can you name some other biblical figures who experienced drastic changes in their lives? How about in your own life? Did God drastically change you?

CHAPTER FOUR

WHAT'S IN A NAME?

Exodus 3:11–22

I n Shakespeare's renowned play *Romeo and Juliet*, the character Juliet makes the following famous inquiry, "What's in a name? That which we call a rose by any other name would smell as sweet." What Juliet is suggesting in that quotation is that what matters is not the name something bears, but rather the essence of the thing itself. Whatever name we put upon a rose has no real impact on its attributes or nature. Essentially, Juliet was stating that names are things indifferent. While there is certainly some truth to Juliet's assertion that names are indifferent when speaking of roses, the same cannot be said when we come to the biblical view of names. In the Bible, a person's name often conveys a great deal about that person and is inseparable from his or her function, nature, calling, and purpose.

Just consider a few examples. Take the name of Abraham, which means "father of a multitude" or "father of many nations." Abraham's name corresponded to his calling and role in God's plan; he was to be the father of many. Another example is the name of Jacob, which means "supplanter." Of course, Jacob lived up to his name when he supplanted his older brother Esau by conniving his way into obtaining his father's blessing. If the meaning of a name is important for human figures in the biblical narrative, how much more is this true when it comes to the name of God.

In the unfolding story of God's relationship with Moses, we are at the point where Moses has just been called to the Herculean task of serving as God's mediator. God has called him to be the human vessel through which God will deliver his people out of bondage to Egypt. Just after receiving this life-changing and challenging calling, Moses makes a request of God; he asks God for his name. God answers this request by sharing his name with Moses—a name that, while short (just four letters in Hebrew), speaks volumes about God's nature, character, and attributes. In this chapter, we will unfold the significance and meaning of the name of God. We will see that, contrary to Juliet's viewpoint, there is much in a name!

THE GOD WHO REVEALS HIMSELF

One of the most striking aspects of the account of God revealing his name to Moses is the fact that God revealed his name to Moses! Think about it for a moment. Here is Moses—a failed prince, a murdering fugitive, and a lowly shepherd—asking God to reveal his name to him. Moses realizes that the task God has given him is great and that the Israelites are likely not to believe anything he says given his past. He is trying to obtain some type of revelation about who God is so that he can use this information with the Israelites to garner some support from the people. Notice how Moses poses the question to God: "Moses said to God, 'Suppose I go to the Israelites and say to them, "The God of your fathers has sent me to you," and they ask me, "What is his name?" Then what shall I tell them?' " (Ex. 3:13). Can you hear the anxiety latent in Moses' question? Can you see how his question reveals a certain level of audacity on Moses' part? After all, Moses is essentially asking the living and powerful God for his calling card!

Moses' anxiety and his inquiry are not surprising. In fact, Moses' actions are entirely understandable and rational, even if they are a bit audacious. The striking part of this encounter is that God actually answers Moses' question. Once again, God stoops down in amazing humility to further the redemption of his people. In an act of intimacy and amazing self-revelation, God tells Moses his name: "God said to Moses, 'I AM WHO I AM.' This is what you are to say to the Israelites: "I AM has sent me to you,"'" (Ex. 3:14).

Now the name that God gave to Moses does speak volumes about who God is, but before we get to the glory of the meaning of his name, it is important to see the glory of the fact that God revealed his name to Moses in the first place. God did not respond to Moses by chastising him for asking such a question. He did not say to Moses, "Who are you to ask me for my name?" Instead, God revealed his name to Moses, and this tells us something about who God is. It tells us that he is the God who reveals himself.

Think about it for a moment. How do you know what God is like? Can you understand who God is from the creation alone? Well, you might be able to understand some of his power and attributes through the creation, as Paul tells us in Romans 1:20, but you could not come to a full understanding of God's plan of redemption by looking at the stars or the trees. The only way we understand God and the plan of salvation is through God's self-revelation in his Word. The Westminster Confession of Faith (WCF) states this truth as follows:

> Although the light of nature, and the works of creation and providence, do so far manifest the goodness, wisdom, and power of God, as to leave men inexcusable; yet are they not sufficient to give that knowledge of God, and of his will, which is necessary unto salvation; therefore it pleased the Lord, at sundry times, and in divers manners, to reveal himself,

and to declare that his will unto his Church; and afterwards for the better preserving and propagating of the truth, and for the more sure establishment and comfort of the Church against the corruption of the flesh, and the malice of Satan and of the world, to commit the same wholly unto writing; which maketh the holy Scripture to be most necessary; those former ways of God's revealing his will unto his people being now ceased. (WCF 1.1)

God must reveal himself and his will to us so that we may know him and his plan of salvation for us. If God had not chosen to reveal himself, we would all be in the dark, lost in an estate of sin and misery.

But the glorious truth of Scripture, which is revealed in this encounter between God and Moses, is that God has not left us in the dark. He reveals himself to us in a myriad of ways and, as the Westminster Confession states, "it pleased the Lord" to reveal himself. Our God is the God who reveals himself.

The Bible is truly God's revelation of himself to us. It displays for us the progressive and unfolding plan of salvation. The Bible recounts how God revealed himself to his people through creation, covenants, dreams, visions, prophets, and, ultimately and most gloriously, through Jesus Christ. Jesus Christ is the greatest self-revelation that God has given us. The writer to the Hebrews captures this point marvelously in the opening verses of that epistle: "In the past God spoke to our ancestors through the prophets at many times and in various ways, but in these last days he has spoken to us by his Son, whom he appointed heir of all things, and through whom also he made the universe" (Heb. 1:1–2).

So the first thing we must marvel at regarding God's name is the fact that he gave it to Moses. This is something that God had not done before, as he himself attests (see Ex. 6:2–3). He chose at this moment, and to this man, to reveal more of himself than he ever had before—he chose to reveal his name. While what Moses experienced was extraordinary, we must always remember that God has revealed his name not merely to one man in history, but, through the proliferation and proclamation of his Word, he has shared that name with each and every one of his children. Even more than that, he has revealed to all his children the name that is above every name—Jesus Christ! He is the God who reveals himself.

THE GOD WHO IS

We have seen that the mere fact that God revealed his name to Moses teaches us something about the nature of God—that he is pleased to reveal himself to us. Now let's begin to explore what the actual name that God gave to Moses reveals about our God. The name God gave to Moses was "I AM WHO I AM." What does this name mean? What does it tell us about God?

There is a link between this name ("I AM"), which is translated as "the Lord," "Jehovah," or "Yahweh," and the Hebrew verb "to be." While the meaning of God's name has broad implications, most scholars agree that one of the things it conveys is the active self-existence and presence of God. He is the God who had no beginning and has no end. He is the God who is self-sufficient and self-determined, owing his existence to no one other than himself. He is the God who *is*.

But there is more to God's name than his declaration of "I AM WHO I AM" found in Exodus 3:14. For instance, in the following verse, God expands on his name: "God also said to Moses, 'Say to the Israelites, "The LORD, the God of your fathers—the God of Abraham, the God of Isaac and the God of Jacob—has sent me to you." This is my name forever, the name you shall call me from generation to generation'" (Ex. 3:15). Whereas the revelation of the name "I AM WHO I AM" spoke to the self-existence of God, the additional self-revelation of God's name in Exodus 3:15 reveals the intimacy and relational aspects of God's character. He is not only the God who is, he is the God who is *with his people*.

In Exodus 3:15, God reveals to Moses that he is "The LORD, the God of your fathers—the God of Abraham, the God of Isaac and the God of Jacob." God had entered into a covenant relationship with Abraham which was to extend throughout Abraham's generations. God was reminding Moses, and by implication the entire nation of Israel, that he is intimately involved with them and that he has not forgotten his covenant made to Abraham. By connecting himself directly with this series of patriarchs—Abraham, Isaac, and Jacob—God demonstrated to Moses that he is an intimate and personal God.

Remember why Moses asked God for his name; he was concerned about his ability to complete his appointed task and was anxious that the Israelites would not receive him because of his checkered past. When God tells Moses that he is the God of Abraham, Isaac, and Jacob, he was telling Moses that he would be with Moses as he had been with those who had preceded him. In other words, God was saying to Moses, "I am the God of Moses."

Through the revelation of his name, God was communicating to Moses that Moses would not be alone in his task. God is the self-existent God who is ever present with his people. He does not forget his people and he will not forsake them. In fact, in Exodus 3:16, God reveals that he has been carefully watching over his people during their time of bondage: "Go, assemble the elders of Israel and say to them, 'The LORD, the God of your fathers—the God of Abraham, Isaac and Jacob—appeared to me and said: *I have watched over you and have seen what has been done to you* in Egypt.'"

By making reference to the patriarchs and by revealing that he has been watching over Israel this entire time, God is telling Moses that he will be with him as he carries out his task as God's mediator. He was reminding Moses that he is the

God who was with Noah during the flood, the God who was with Abraham at Mount Moriah, and the God who was with Joseph during his imprisonment in Egypt. God was assuring and comforting Moses; he was reaffirming what he said to him in Exodus 3:12: "And God said, *'I will be with you.* And this will be the sign to you that it is I who have sent you: When you have brought the people out of Egypt, you will worship God on this mountain.'" God was informing Moses that he would not be alone. As Michael D. Williams notes, contextually within Exodus 3:13–15, the name "I AM THAT I AM may well be taken as 'I will be to you as I was to them' (the fathers of Ex. 3:13), or 'I will be there—with you in Egypt—as I am here.'"[1] Moses knew he would not be alone.

Once again, what Moses learned about God from his name is not limited in its application to Moses alone. While the promise of God's enduring presence had a unique application in the life of Moses as God's mediator, it is a promise that is shared by every person who is under God's covenantal care. The promise in Hebrews 13:5 is for every child of God: "Never will I leave you; never will I forsake you." Particularly in the era of the new covenant, the church enjoys the promise of Jesus' enduring presence with his people as he promised in the Great Commission: "And surely I am with you always, to the very end of the age" (Matt. 28:20). Our God is the God who is and the God who is with us. Nowhere is this promise more tangibly felt than in the incarnation of Jesus Christ. The promise of Isaiah 7:14 makes this clear: "Therefore the Lord himself will give you a sign: The virgin will conceive and give birth to a son, and will call him Immanuel." God was not only with Abraham, Isaac, Jacob, and Moses—he is God with *us*!

THE GOD WHO KEEPS HIS PROMISES

When God revealed his name to Moses, he also revealed additional aspects of his character that are intimately connected to his name. His name not only expresses metaphysical realities about God's self-existence, self-sufficiency, and his active presence with his people, it also has covenantal and historical importance. God associates his name with his covenant promises and his mighty acts in history. He places his name upon significant historical places and items—the ark, the tabernacle, and the temple. These covenantal and historical aspects of God's name appear to be the main emphasis in God's revelation of his name to Moses. As Michael D. Williams writes, "While there may be some claim of existence in the name Yahweh it is the covenantal and historical reality of God that is fundamentally at issue in the name Yahweh."[2] The main thing that God was communicating to Moses in revealing his name is that he is the God who keeps his covenant promises.

After God revealed his name to Moses, he gave further instructions to Moses regarding how to proceed. Essentially, God gave Moses a script to use when speaking to the Israelites. Note how God grounds his actions in delivering the Israelites in his promise:

> "Go, assemble the elders of Israel and say to them, 'The Lord, the God of your fathers—the God of Abraham, Isaac and Jacob—appeared to me and said: I have watched over you and have seen what has been done to you in Egypt. And *I have promised to bring you up out of your misery in Egypt* into the land of the Canaanites, Hittites, Amorites, Perizzites, Hivites and Jebusites—a land flowing with milk and honey.' " (Ex. 3:16–17.)

Everything in this script is grounded in history ("the God of your fathers—the God of Abraham, Isaac and Jacob") and covenant ("And I have promised to bring you up out of your misery in Egypt"). God's name is associated with his mighty acts in history.

What God was about to do in delivering the Israelites from bondage to the Egyptians was not a new idea, but grounded in history and covenant. As God was unfolding his covenant promise to Abraham (then "Abram") in Genesis 15, God informed Abraham that his descendants would be in bondage to the Egyptians,

> As the sun was setting, Abram fell into a deep sleep, and a thick and dreadful darkness came over him. Then the LORD said to him, "Know for certain that for four hundred years your descendants will be strangers in a country not their own and that they will be enslaved and mistreated there." (Gen. 15:12–13)

But God also promised Abraham that this enslavement and mistreatment would end: "But I will punish the nation they serve as slaves, and afterward they will come out with great possessions" (Gen. 15:14). This promise of deliverance from Egypt was later reiterated to the patriarch Jacob.

> And God spoke to Israel in a vision at night and said, "Jacob! Jacob!"
>
> "Here I am," he replied.
>
> "I am God, the God of your father," he said. "Do not be afraid to go down to Egypt, for I will make you into a great nation there. *I will go down to Egypt with you, and I will surely bring you back again.* And Joseph's own hand will close your eyes." (Gen. 46:2–4)

God promised to bring back his people and Moses was enlisted as the human agent through which God would fulfill this promise.

The name that God gave to Moses is his covenant name. It is a name that reminds us that God acts in history to keep his covenant promises. Moses had the assurance and comfort of knowing that the promise-keeping God was going with him. He had the knowledge that God was not only the God of the historical Abraham, Isaac, Jacob, and Joseph, but he was also the God of Moses.

The comfort that Moses had in the knowledge that he was serving the promise-keeping God who places his covenant name as a seal upon his promise is a comfort that all believers share. In our world there are so many broken promises; this is such a painful aspect of our existence. If you have ever had a friend, spouse, employer, or parent break a promise, then you well understand the grief this action causes. The joy we have as believers is that we serve a God who never forgets or breaks his promises. The victory of Jesus Christ on the cross is evidence of how far our God will go to fulfill his promises to us. As the apostle Paul reminds us, every single promise God has made is affirmed in the work of Jesus Christ: "For no matter how many promises God has made, they are 'Yes' in Christ. And so through him the 'Amen' is spoken by us to the glory of God" (2 Cor. 1:20). God's name reveals that he is a God who keeps his promises.

THE GOD WHO IS ALL-POWERFUL

So far we have seen that God's sharing of his name with Moses provided great comfort to Moses because God's name reminded Moses that God would be present with him and that God keeps his promises. Moses knew that he would not be alone in his task, and he knew that he could rest upon God's faithfulness to the covenant made with Abraham. But there is yet another comforting truth that God shared with Moses in the context of revealing his name; God revealed that he is the all-powerful God.

The reason this revelation was important to Moses was that he was about to take on the mighty Pharaoh, his magicians, and his army. While having the revelation of God's covenant promise to deliver his people was certainly comforting to Moses, it was even more comforting for him to know that God had the power to fulfill that promise. God demonstrated this fact to Moses in two ways.

He did so first by demonstrating that he had knowledge of future events. In other words, God showed Moses that he knew exactly what would happen—that he knew the end from the beginning. For example, in Exodus 3:18, God revealed that he knew how the elders of Israel would respond to God's message delivered through Moses: "The elders of Israel will listen to you." God assured Moses that his message would be heeded and that Moses would not be rejected. God also revealed that he knew exactly how Pharaoh would respond to Moses' demand for the Israelites to be freed: "But I know that the king of Egypt will not let you go unless a mighty hand compels him" (Ex. 3:19). God demonstrated to Moses that he knows all things. He is, as the theologians put it, omniscient; he knows everything.

The second way that God revealed his awesome power to Moses was by his declaration that he would stretch out his hand against the Egyptians and perform wonders among them (Ex. 3:20). This imagery is rife with the ferocious power of God. This anthropomorphic language of God stretching out his arm conveyed to Moses that God would be the divine warrior in this battle. Moses would not need an army to oppose Pharaoh because he had the mighty outstretched arm of the living, active, and all-powerful God on his side! God is not only omniscient, but he is also omnipotent. He is the Great I Am!

As I write this book, our nation is in the midst of another presidential election. Elections are replete with promises. Candidates offer endless platitudes and promises to solve our nation's problems. Most people count these promises as what they all too frequently are—empty promises. Very few politicians actually deliver on their promises. Part of the reason why they can't is that they simply lack the power to bring their agendas to fruition by themselves. When it comes to God, however, there are no empty promises. When God makes a promise he backs it up with his power to fulfill it. He is the God who can create all things out of nothing, flood the earth, part the Red Sea, and topple the walls of Jericho. Through the incarnate Son of God, God once again displays his almighty power as Jesus heals the sick and raises the dead. Even greater than all these amazing demonstrations of his power is the reality that through the death and resurrection of Jesus Christ, God displays his power to conquer sin and death.

God showed Moses that his name has power. Moses would one day see that power displayed in the parting of the Red Sea. After seeing God's mighty outstretched arm striking the Egyptians on that day, Moses led Israel in a song that included these words, "Who among the gods is like you, LORD? Who is like you—majestic in holiness, awesome in glory, working wonders?" (Ex. 15:11). The reality of God's omnipotence should fill all of us with great comfort, joy, and assurance. God has the power, evidenced by the completed work of Jesus Christ, to deliver us fully from our sins, from death, and from the sentence that once hung over our heads that required us to face the wrath of that very same all-powerful God. Our only hope for salvation is found in the name of the Great I Am!

THE GREAT I AM!

As we have seen in this chapter, when God revealed his name to Moses he also revealed volumes regarding his nature, character, and attributes. Through the revelation of his name, God demonstrated that he is the God who reveals himself, the God who is, the God who keeps his promises, and the God who is all-powerful.

In addition, by revealing his name, God also revealed a bit about his *modus operandi* (or "method of operation"). As we've seen, God's name is revealed in the context of history and covenant. He is the God of Abraham, Isaac, and Jacob. These are historical figures, and God related to them through his covenant promises, which he made in history. The entire exodus event is grounded in God's covenant promises made to Abraham hundreds of years earlier. God was delivering Israel from Egypt because they were his covenant people and he promised to deliver them.

God's name reveals so much about him. It is amazing to think about how much information is conveyed through two words and three letters—I AM. Of course, this first revelation of God's name in Exodus finds its organic and progressive fulfillment in the coming of Jesus Christ.

First, think of the name "Jesus." It means "God saves." The angel of the Lord commanded Joseph to give Jesus this name: "She will give birth to a son, and you are to give him the name Jesus, because he will save his people from their sins" (Matt. 1:21). Jesus' name tells us about his mission and purpose.

But there is more to the name of Jesus. The New Testament reminds us in numerous places of the power of asking and praying in the name of Jesus. As Jesus told his disciples in John 14:13, "And I will do whatever you ask in my name, so that the Father may be glorified in the Son." The New Testament also speaks of the eschatological judgment power of Jesus' name:

> Therefore God exalted him to the highest place and gave him the name that is above every name, that at the name of Jesus every knee should bow, in heaven and on earth and under the earth, and every tongue acknowledge that Jesus Christ is Lord, to the glory of God the Father. (Phil. 2:9–11)

Jesus' name not only describes his mission, but it also reflects his lordship, divinity, and power.

While all of these aspects of Jesus' name reflect his divinity and honor as the Son of God, there was one moment in his ministry that is a direct corollary to the revelation of God's name in Exodus. During one of Jesus' exchanges with the Pharisees, Jesus spoke of Abraham seeing Jesus' day and rejoicing in it (John 8:56); this set the Pharisees into a fury. "The Jews then said to him, 'You are not yet fifty years old, and have you seen Abraham?'" (John 8:57). Jesus replied with these powerful words reminiscent of Exodus 3:14: "Jesus said to them, 'Truly, truly! I say to you, before Abraham was, I AM.'" What was Jesus saying here? He was saying what God was saying to Moses in Exodus 3:14. Jesus was declaring that he is the self-existent and all-powerful God. It's no wonder that the Jews who heard these words wanted to kill him for uttering them.

Like Moses and the Israelites, outside of Jesus Christ we are all subject to bondage. Our bondage is not to the Egyptians, but rather to sin and death. Jesus, the Great I Am, has delivered us from this death. His name reminds us that he has the power to keep his covenant promises to us. His name reminds us that he has set us free. When it comes to Jesus, there is much in a name!

FOR FURTHER REFLECTION

1. This chapter focuses on the importance and meaning of God's name. Why are names important in the Bible?
2. When Moses asked God for his name, God graciously responded by sharing it with Moses. What does this reveal about how God relates to us and how we can know him?
3. What does the revelation of God's name ("I AM") reveal about his nature, character, and attributes?
4. When God revealed his name to Moses, he made reference to the patriarchs. What did this communicate to Moses about God's relationship with him and Israel as a nation?

5. God revealed his covenant name to Moses and showed himself as a God who keeps his promises. Can you list some promises God has made to us in the Bible? How can the reality of God's faithfulness to his promises be used to witness to the world around us?

6. How does God's name reveal his power?

7. How does the revelation of God's name point us to the person and work of Jesus Christ?

CHAPTER FIVE

THE GOD WHO IS
SUFFICIENT

Exodus 4:1–17

T he Oscar winning film *The King's Speech* tells the story of Albert Frederick Arthur George, the man who eventually became King George VI of England. Albert ("Bertie") did not expect to become king. He only did so because his brother, Edward, abdicated the throne to marry a divorced American woman. Albert had always lived in his brother's shadow, but with his ascension to the throne, the spotlight was now on him. Albert had another problem: he was plagued by a stammer. He had become the king of England in 1936 during the build-up toward World War II. He would be tested by the onslaught of Adolph Hitler and Nazi Germany. He would have to speak to his nation through radio addresses. What type of confidence would a stammering king give to his people? The movie tells the remarkable story of how King George VI overcame his verbal obstacles through the help of an unorthodox speech therapist named Lionel Logue. By means of Logue's assistance, King George VI was able to speak and lead his people through a time of great trial.

Like King George VI, Moses was about to lead his people through a tremendous trial. Moses had been enlisted by

God to be his leader and mouthpiece. He had been called by God to confront the mightiest military and political power on earth. But like King George VI, Moses felt utterly inadequate, insufficient, and ill-equipped for the task. In this chapter, we will see how Moses voices his insufficiencies and how God demonstrates to Moses that he is the God who is sufficient.

THE INSUFFICIENCY OF MOSES

One of the things about the Bible that provides me a great deal of encouragement is how honest it is about its heroes. This is really a testimony to the inspired nature of revelation. Most solely human histories tend to engage in a level of hagiography (or "saint making") when it comes to telling the story of national heroes. The Bible is not like that; it portrays its heroes truthfully—warts and all. This gives me encouragement because I have plenty of insufficiencies myself. The fact that God enlisted people in his service who were far from perfect gives me great hope that I can be useful in his kingdom. As we look at Moses' insufficiencies, you will likely share at least some of them. Let it be an encouragement to you that God can use flawed and insufficient people like Moses, and you, and me!

In Exodus 3, Moses received God's calling on his life to lead the liberation of the Israelites from Egypt. But as the story turns to Exodus 4, we see Moses' personal struggle with this calling. He perceives the task as too great, and all he can see are his own failings. Moses is certain that he will fail because of his own weakness.

Insecurity

Moses' struggle with his own insufficiencies begins in the very first verse of Exodus 4 as he turns to God and inquires, "What if they do not believe me or listen to me and say, 'The Lord did not appear to you'?" (Ex. 4:1).

Here Moses reveals his own insecurities and lack of self-confidence. Moses feared that he lacked the integrity and credibility with the Israelites to complete his mission. He feared they would reject him—and indeed there was some warrant for his fears.

There were at least four good reasons for Moses to feel insecure about the Israelites accepting him as their leader and liberator. First, it had been forty years since his last contact with his enslaved Hebrew brethren. He had to wonder whether anyone would even remember him. Second, if they did actually remember him, then they would recall that his exit from Egypt was a shameful one. Moses had left Egypt a fugitive from a murder charge. He had to wonder whether anyone would accept him as a leader given his checkered and shameful past. A third reason they might reject him is because he had spent the last forty years in utter obscurity as a shepherd in a backwater town. He had to wonder whether anyone would think he, a second-rate shepherd, was qualified to do battle with Pharaoh. Finally, Moses had reason to be insecure about his acceptance because he was about to tell the Israelites that God had met him in a burning bush that was not consumed and told Moses that his name was "I AM." He had to wonder whether they would think he was absolutely out of his mind.

Moses had good reason to feel insecure about being accepted in his new role. But this was not the only inadequacy that Moses was experiencing as he contemplated the task before him.

Incompetence

In addition to feeling insecure about his reception by the Israelites, Moses also felt like he was not equipped for the task. Moses questioned his competency for the role of liberator and leader. Like King George VI, Moses felt particularly incompetent to be a spokesperson. "Pardon your servant, Lord. I have never been eloquent, neither in the past nor since you have spoken to your servant. I am slow of speech and tongue" (Ex. 4:10). God had called Moses to a task that required him to exercise a gift that he perceived he did not possess—the gift of oration. Moses was struggling with the fear of failure which flowed from his sense of being incompetent for the task set before him.

Struggling with Our Weaknesses

It is easy to be critical of Moses' seeming lack of faith as seen in this text. After all, God had appeared to him and spoke to him out of a burning bush. What else does he need? How can he be fearful and faithless in the face of such glorious and personal revelation? But we should not rush to judgment here. Moses was human just like us. I can recall many times in my life when my sense of insufficiency, insecurity, and incompetence have led me to desire to run away from a calling. Have you ever pleaded with God to just send someone else? My guess is that, if you are anything like me, you have.

So what do we do when we feel like running from God's calling due to our insufficiencies? We remind ourselves that fulfilling God's calling is not about our sufficiency for the task; rather, it is about God's sufficiency. We need to remember that it is not about our weaknesses, but about God's strength. This is exactly what God revealed to Moses as Moses struggled with his sense of insufficiency. God told Moses that he is the God who is sufficient.

THE GOD WHO IS SUFFICIENT

As we read through Moses' series of complaints regarding why he could not do what God was asking of him, we see God answering each enumerated complaint of Moses with a response that calls Moses to rely upon God rather than himself.

Empowered to Serve

Consider, for example, Moses' fear that no one would listen to him or believe that he was God's spokesman (Ex. 4:1). God replied to Moses' insecurity by giving him a demonstration of his power. Note God's response in Exodus 4:2–8:

> Then the LORD said to him, "What is that in your hand?"
>
> "A staff," he replied.
>
> The LORD said, "Throw it on the ground."
>
> Moses threw it on the ground and it became a snake, and he ran from it. Then the LORD said to him, "Reach out your hand and take it by the tail." So Moses reached out and took hold of the snake and it turned back into a staff in his hand. "This," said the LORD, "is so that they may believe that the LORD, the God of their fathers—the God of Abraham, the God of Isaac and the God of Jacob—has appeared to you."
>
> Then the LORD said, "Put your hand inside your cloak." So Moses put his hand into his cloak, and when he took it out, the skin was leprous—it had become as white as snow.
>
> "Now put it back into your cloak," he said. So Moses put his hand back into his cloak, and when he took it out, it was restored, like the rest of his flesh.
>
> Then the LORD said, "If they do not believe you or pay attention to the first sign, they may believe the second. But if they do not believe these two signs or listen to you, take some water from the Nile and pour it on the dry ground. The water you take from the river will become blood on the ground."

God countered Moses' insecurity through a series of visible demonstrations of God's power. God promised to authenticate Moses' ministry through signs and wonders. In other words, God would back up Moses' words with his own mighty deeds.

In the Bible, signs and wonders are never merely random or arbitrary displays of God's power. Nor does God, as C. S. Lewis put it, "perform parlor tricks." God employs signs and wonders as a means of confirming the veracity of his Word and promises. This is exactly how Jesus used signs in his ministry—to confirm his Word, authenticate his role as the Messiah, and teach people about the nature and power of God. Of course, unlike Moses, Jesus performed his signs and wonders in his own divine power.

But the power of these signs was not merely in the fact that God promises to perform them; there was also a message being conveyed through the nature of the signs themselves. God promised to perform three signs—turning a staff into a snake, making a healthy hand leprous, and changing the water from the Nile into blood. Each of these signs was designed to strike at the heart of Egyptian pride and power. For instance, the cobra was an important symbol in Egypt; it was so important that it was used on the crown of Pharaoh. The cobra's national significance to Egypt compares to the national significance of the bald eagle to the United States. Accordingly, the turning of a staff to a snake carried the not-so-subtle message that God was sovereign over Egypt. The second sign, the hand becoming leprous, also struck at the heart of Egypt's power. During this time leprosy was rampant in Egypt; this sign conveyed that God was sovereign over this disease that was ravaging Egypt's population. God's sovereignty over leprosy is a theme that runs throughout redemptive history. Leprosy rendered a person ceremonially unclean and thus unfit to be in God's presence. There were times when God inflicted this disease upon people as punishment, as he did with the Egyptians, and other times when he healed people, like Naaman, of this disease (2 Kings 5:1–14). In the New Testament, we see Jesus exercising sovereignty over the disease as he heals lepers, thereby making clean those who were formerly unclean (Matt. 8:1–4; Luke 17:11–19).

The last sign God promised to perform, the turning of the water of the Nile into blood, was really the trump card of these signs. For Egypt, the Nile was life itself. The Nile was central to Egypt's food supply and national economy. The Nile sustained the nation. By turning the water of the Nile into blood, God was stating that he could destroy this life-sustaining water and Egypt along with it. But there is more to this final sign than simply establishing God's sovereignty over the waters of the Nile. By turning the Nile into blood, God was directly challenging both the divine claims of the Pharaoh and the alleged power of the pantheon of the Egyptian gods. At least three Egyptian gods (Khnum, Hapi, and Osiris) were connected to the Nile; God demonstrated their impotence by turning its waters to blood.

God's promise of signs and wonders provided Moses with great security that his people would not only receive him, but also that he would ultimately prevail over Egyptian power. God promised Moses that God himself would endorse Moses' ministry with divine authentication. Moses' insecurity was answered with the sufficiency of God's power.

Equipped to Serve

We have seen that, in addition to feeling insecure, Moses also felt incompetent. In Exodus 4:10, Moses expresses that he has "never been eloquent" and that he is "slow of speech and tongue." Once again, God answers Moses' sense of insufficiency with a promise of his own sufficiency: "The LORD said to him, 'Who gave human beings their mouths? Who makes them deaf or mute? Who gives them sight or makes them blind? Is it not I, the LORD?' " (Ex. 4:11). With these words God reminded Moses that God was the one who had created the mouth, the tongue, and language itself. Implicit in this declaration of God's sovereignty over speech is a promise to Moses that God can give him the words to say.

But God was not finished addressing Moses' sense of incompetence with regard to his speech. In the following verse, Exodus 4:12, God makes the implicit promise of Exodus 4:11 explicit with this further promise to Moses: "Now go; I will help you speak and will teach you what to say." God promised to be Moses' teacher, to give him the words that would be necessary to accomplish his mission. In an interesting parallel, Jesus makes a similar promise to his own disciples as they are nearing the time of carrying out the Great Commission and facing the prospect of doing this without Jesus being with them:

parallel

> All this I have spoken while still with you. But the Advocate, the Holy Spirit, whom the Father will send in my name, *will teach you all things and will remind you of everything I have said to you.* Peace I leave with you; my peace I give you. I do not give to you as the world gives. Do not let your hearts be troubled and do not be afraid. (John 14:25–27)

God answered Moses' sense of incompetency by reminding him that God was not asking him to do this in his own power or to make up his own words. Instead, God promised to equip Moses for the task and to give him the words that would not return void. Moses' sense of incompetence was answered with the sufficiency of God's equipping power.

God responded to Moses' insufficiencies by reminding Moses of God's power. He never denied the reality of Moses' insufficiencies. In fact, the signs that God gave to Moses only served to further reveal them. For example, Moses displays his fear as he runs from the snake that was formerly his staff, and he is rendered ceremonially unclean by the leprosy he contracted from sticking his hand in the cloak. God wanted Moses to see and understand his insufficiencies, but he also wanted Moses to know that God is sufficient to make up for those insufficiencies. He reminded Moses that he is the God who is sufficient for our needs.

A QUESTION OF FOCUS

When we boil down this exchange between God and Moses we see that Moses' real problem here was not that he had insufficiencies, but that his focus was on his insufficiencies rather than upon God. In essence, when we wallow in what we lack, we are actually being self-centered. This is what Moses was doing. He was trying to measure up to God's calling when he should have realized that he could never do so in his own strength. Moses needed to be refocused upon God.

We can witness Moses' self-centered focus in his exchange with God in Exodus 4. After God had promised to perform signs and wonders and teach Moses what to say, Moses was still focusing upon himself. Even in the wake of these great promises Moses declared, "Pardon your servant, Lord. Please send someone else" (Ex. 4:13).

Although it is impossible to know exactly what Moses was thinking here, it seems likely there were at least two dynamics at work here. First, his words in Exodus 4:13 may have been a last ditch plea based on Moses' sense of his insufficiency for the task set before him. But I think there is something else going on here. Moses' words also display fear, stubbornness, recalcitrance, lack of faithfulness, and his self-centeredness. After all of God's promises, Moses is still focusing on himself and his insufficiencies. God was not pleased. In Exodus 4:14 we learn that "the Lord's anger burned against Moses." In the verses that follow, God graciously offers Aaron to serve as Moses' mouthpiece, once again displaying to Moses that God's power is sufficient. But while God was gracious to Moses, it is clear that God was angry that Moses was still focused on his own inadequacies rather than on God's power.

The mistake Moses made here is not unfamiliar to us. We are ever tempted to be focused improperly on our own strengths or weaknesses. Either way, whether we are feeling self-sufficient or insufficient, we are making the mistake of focusing on self rather than upon God. All that we do in God's kingdom is empowered by him. God's plan simply does not depend upon us. Our sufficiency is found in Jesus Christ. This is a lesson that Moses had to learn, and it is one that we need to learn, and continually relearn, as well.

THE SUFFICIENCY OF CHRIST

Living up to God's calling and standards is an impossible task in our own strength. Moses realized this as he was assessing facing Pharaoh in his own strength. But there is a calling that God places on all of our lives that is even more challenging than leading the Israelites out of Egypt. In Leviticus 19:2 and 1 Peter 1:16 we read of this calling: "Be holy, because I am holy." How sufficient do you feel in the face of that calling?

The Scriptures unequivocally teach that we, in our natural state, are utterly insufficient when it comes to holiness and righteousness. What precipitated this insufficiency? The sin of our first parents, Adam and Eve, and all the sins we have wrought through our own personal disobedience to God's moral law precipitated this insufficiency. There was a reason why God stationed cherubim with flaming swords to guard the garden of Eden; it is holy ground and the unholy, meaning humanity, cannot dwell within its confines. As Paul reminds us in Romans 3:10, echoing Psalm 14, "As it is written: 'There is no one righteous, not even one.'" This is our core insufficiency as humans: a lack of personal holiness and righteousness. This is what disqualifies us from God's presence. It was this lack of personal righteousness which led the psalmist to inquire rhetorically:

Who may ascend the mountain of the LORD?
 Who may stand in his holy place?
The one who has clean hands and a pure heart,
 who does not trust in an idol or swear by a false
  god. (Ps. 24:2–3)

Here the psalmist is probing at the most essential question of human existence. Who may dwell in the presence of God? The answer is only the one who possesses perfect righteousness—who has clean hands and a pure heart.

Based on the standard of Psalm 24, every human after our first parents is unable to stand in the holy place. We are all utterly insufficient. This is the core dilemma of humanity—God requires perfect holiness and we lack it. How are we able to escape this dilemma? We do exactly what Moses eventually did. We turn our eyes away from ourselves and our own insufficiencies to the God who is sufficient, particularly to the person of Jesus Christ.

Jesus Christ is the answer to the psalmist's rhetorical question voiced in Psalm 24. Jesus, and Jesus alone, is the one who can ascend the hill of the Lord and stand in his holy place. Why? Because Jesus alone has clean hands and a pure heart—he alone has perfect righteousness. Jesus alone is sufficient.

Ultimately, our sufficiency is found in the person and work of Jesus Christ. He has eclipsed the insufficient priesthood of the Old Testament by making one sufficient sacrifice for all our sins, as the writer to the Hebrews states:

Now there have been many of those priests, since death prevented them from continuing in office; but because Jesus lives forever, he has a permanent priesthood. Therefore he is able to save completely those who come to God through him, because he always lives to intercede for them.
 Such a high priest truly meets our need—one who is holy, blameless, pure, set apart from sinners,

exalted above the heavens. Unlike the other high priests, he does not need to offer sacrifices day after day, first for his own sins, and then for the sins of the people. He sacrificed for their sins once for all when he offered himself. (Heb. 7:23–27)

As the writer to the Hebrews notes in this passage, we have a "high priest [who] truly meets our need." We have a high priest who is sufficient for our salvation. He is "holy, blameless, pure, set apart from sinners, exalted above the heavens." How can we ascend the hill of the Lord and stand in his holy place? There is only one answer to that question—through Jesus Christ.

Just as Moses learned, we must continually be reminded that our sufficiency is not found in ourselves. This is so vitally important for us to grasp, particularly when it comes to our salvation. In the sphere of redemption, we are so insufficient that we do not contribute anything to our salvation. Salvation is not about what we do, it is about what God has done. Paul makes this very point in 2 Timothy 1:9: "He has saved us and called us to a holy life—not because of anything we have done but *because of his own purpose and grace.*" Paul goes on in that text to remind us that Jesus' work in redemption is so sufficient that it provides us the assurance that he will complete that work in our lives. Paul states his confidence in Christ in 1 Timothy 1:12: "because I know whom I have believed, and am *convinced that he is able to guard what I have entrusted to him* until that day."

While Moses was worried about his insufficiencies to carry out the calling that God had placed on his life, his most pressing insufficiency was his inability to stand righteous before a holy God. God properly refocused the eyes and heart of Moses. God turned Moses from himself to God as the provider. The entire exodus event reiterates this point to Moses, the Israelites, and even to us today. God will bring his people out of bondage in Egypt. He does it in his power and his timing. He is the God who is sufficient.

As believers we have many callings. We fill roles as children, parents, spouses, and employees. We need to look to God for strength and sufficiency in all of these areas of our lives. But the most important calling we have is to be holy. This demands that we look to the Christ who is sufficient, that we look to him "who is able to do immeasurably more than all we ask or imagine, according to his power that is at work within us" (Eph. 3:20).

FOR FURTHER REFLECTION

1. What was the nature of Moses' insecurity regarding his calling?
2. How did God provide reassurance to Moses regarding his insecurities?
3. Why did Moses feel incompetent regarding his calling?
4. How did God provide reassurance to Moses regarding his incompetency?
5. What was Moses' main mistake with regard to his evaluating his sufficiency for the calling God gave to him?
6. How does Psalm 24 point us to Jesus Christ and focus us on Christ's sufficiency for us?

CHAPTER SIX

THE PROPHET, THE PHARAOH, AND THE PLAGUES

Exodus 5–11

W hy do bad things happen to good people? Why do people do bad things? These two questions have empowered atheists and challenged believers for millennia. Every time an earthquake, hurricane, or some other disaster strikes the United States there will inevitably emerge a theologian or televangelist who claims to have the explanation for the cause of the catastrophe. Often the reason given is the moral decadence of the nation. Similarly, when a person engages in an evil act such as a mass shooting, there will arise a pundit or psychologist who claims to have the explanation for what triggered this event. Typically, the explanation includes the childhood experiences of the perpetrator or the idea that he was influenced by violence on television, in movies, or in video games.

Offering answers to these two questions is a precarious task. We simply lack specific knowledge of God's will with regard to such historical events. We know general principles that we can apply to these events, but we don't know exactly why God allowed a specific disaster or evil act to occur. There are aspects of God's will that are not revealed to us, as Deuteronomy 29:29 reminds us: "The secret things belong to the LORD our God." Accordingly, we must always be careful in daring to proffer answers to these two questions when it comes to events and actions in our world.

This does not mean, however, that the Bible is without guidance regarding answering such questions. The Bible often allows us to see various historical events and actions through the eyes of God. We are sometimes given a divine perspective on why God allowed or caused certain events to happen. These moments are incredibly valuable in discerning why bad things sometimes happen to good people and why people do bad things. Yet, though such divine insights cannot necessarily be applied directly to explain God's purposes regarding specific events in our own time, they are nonetheless useful in helping us to understand these events and to trust in God as we experience them.

In this chapter, we will explore one of those extraordinary divine perspectives that give us incredible insight into these two fundamental questions. We will witness a nation being assailed by a series of disasters and a leader who, despite these disasters, exacerbates the suffering of his people by repeatedly refusing to choose what is good and right. We will learn about the prophet, the plagues, and the Pharaoh, but most of all we will learn about the power and mercy of God.

THE PROPHET

As Moses' great confrontation with Pharaoh is drawing near, we must recognize that he has come a long way. Moses has traversed the spectrum from being a spoiled, prideful, and privileged son in Pharaoh's house to living as a humble shepherd in Midian, to being a hesitant and reluctant servant at the burning bush, and, finally, now, to serving as a faithful prophet and son in God's house. As he stands on the eve of the great battle with Egypt, he is a changed man. He is confident in his God, in his cause, and in his people's ultimate victory.

The character of this new Moses can be seen in how he approaches the leader of the most powerful nation of his time. Moses and Aaron approach the throne of Pharaoh and they do not quiver, waver, or grovel; instead they proclaim to this mighty leader, "This is what the Lord, the God of Israel, says: 'Let my people go, so that they may hold a festival to me in the wilderness'" (Ex. 5:1). This was an incredibly bold act. Moses and Aaron were risking their very lives to make such a demand upon Pharaoh, but they did it without compromise. Note also what is absent from their words. There is no Moses in these words. Moses, at least at this moment, realizes that God's liberation of his people will occur through God's power, not his own.

Moses had lost his fear and self-centeredness. He is now confident and focused on God's power. What accounts for this transformation in his life? Moses was changed by the revelation of God. Moses had met the living God. He met him in the dark and lonely moments in the deserts of Midian where Moses repented of his pride and began to die to self. He met the living God at the burning bush where he heard the Great I Am proclaim a message of liberation regarding his people. As Moses and Aaron state in Exodus 5:3, "The God of the Hebrews has met with us." What changed Moses was God himself.

The type of powerful transformation that we witness in Moses is paralleled in the New Testament and the ministry of Jesus. Consider, for example, the character of Jesus' disciples in the early part of his ministry. They come across as impulsive, dim-witted, and weak in the knees. They don't quite understand what the kingdom of God is about and they often completely fail to grasp who Jesus really is. Even at the crucifixion they still seem dense and frightful.

Think of Peter's threefold denial of Jesus. But then these seemingly incompetent disciples become bold spokesmen of the gospel, even in the face of the Roman and Jewish authorities. They risk life and limb to advance the cause of Christ and expand the boundaries of the church. What happened to them? What accounts for their miraculous transformation? They met the living Christ and were filled with the Holy Spirit. They met the Great I Am.

Though we are not called as prophets or apostles in the same sense as Moses or Jesus' apostles, there is a parallel to the transformation that God brought about in their lives and the transformation he works in every one of his children. The Scriptures reveal that God takes great pleasure in what some theologians refer to as "redemptive irony." God enjoys using the foolish things to confound the wise and using weak things to shame the strong (1 Cor. 1:27). He took a fearful fugitive like Moses and turned him into the mediator of the old covenant and leader of his people. He grabbed the runt of the litter in David and made him the greatest of Israel's Old Testament kings. He commenced his plan for the salvation of his people through a baby born in a manger. He sealed the salvation of his people through what seemed to the world a defeat of his own Son on the cross. This pattern of redemptive irony is present in every believer's life. God takes foolish people like us and makes us his children. He takes those who were at enmity with him and makes them his servants. Like Moses and the apostles, every believer is transformed by the power of the living God.

When the prophet Moses approached the throne of Pharaoh he came as a changed man. He did not come to negotiate. He came with a simple command that was not based on his own authority, but rather on the authority of the living God. He conveyed to Pharaoh the demand of God, "Let my people go." Now it was Pharaoh's turn to encounter the power of the living God. How would he respond? Would he be transformed like Moses? Would he have a change of heart and obey the demand of God? We have seen what happened in the heart of the prophet Moses, but what will happen in the heart of Pharaoh?

THE PHARAOH

As we have seen, Moses' heart has been on a spiritual journey from love of self to love of God. Moses' faith has increased through his interaction with God, as has his willingness to trust and serve him. When it comes to Pharaoh's story, we witness the exact opposite dynamic. Pharaoh's heart begins like Moses' heart, hardened by self-love and pride, but, unlike in the case of Moses, Pharaoh's heart proceeds on a path of further calcification. Pharaoh's heart never softens; rather, it becomes increasingly resistant to God's love and will.

We can witness the starting point of Pharaoh's heart in the very first encounter he has with Moses and Aaron. When they come to Pharaoh in Exodus 5:1 they make the following demand upon him: "This is what the LORD, the God of Israel, says: 'Let my people go, so that they may hold a festival to me in the wilderness.'" God was not yet demanding the full liberation of his people in this statement. Instead, he was telling Pharaoh to allow his people to have the freedom to worship him for three days in the wilderness. Pharaoh responded to this demand with contempt, "Who is the LORD, that I should obey him and let Israel go? I do not know the LORD and I will not let Israel go" (Ex. 5:2).

Now at first we may look at Pharaoh's reply and desire to condemn him on the spot for disregarding God's message, but such a knee-jerk reaction would be unfair. The key phrase in Pharaoh's response comes when he declares that he does not "know the LORD." This was a true statement. Pharaoh had not previously encountered God or his message. In many ways, he was just like the rest of us in this regard. When I first heard God's message through the Scriptures, I had a similar reaction to its claims on my life. Like Pharaoh, I said in my heart, "Who is the Lord, that I should obey him?" and "I do not know the Lord." Every person who does not know God begins in the very position that Pharaoh occupied—inclined not to accept God's truth. But God was not done with Pharaoh. This was just the beginning.

God responded to Pharaoh's confession of ignorance of him by unleashing a series of events that were meant to ensure that Pharaoh and Egypt would "know the LORD." Between Exodus 5 and Exodus 11 God will declare numerous times that the purpose of his actions are so that Pharaoh and Egypt will "know the LORD" (Ex. 7:5, 17; 8:10, 22; 9:14, 16, 29; 10:2). The first four chapters of the book of Exodus told the story of God's revelation of himself to Moses. This section is the story of God's revelation of himself to Pharaoh. The intriguing part of the story is the stark polarity in how these two men, Moses and Pharaoh, respond to that revelation.

The main way that God reveals himself to Pharaoh is through the performance of signs and wonders. God brings a series of plagues upon Egypt in an effort to reveal his power to Pharaoh and his people. We will explore some of the theological meaning of the particular plagues and why God used them, but here we will focus upon the reaction of Pharaoh to this revelation. We saw in Exodus 5:2 that he begins this journey with an ignorant and resistant heart, just like all of us begin our respective journeys. Now let's see what happens to his heart as God reveals himself through the power of the plagues.

As each successive plague comes upon Egypt, Pharaoh's heart has only one reaction—it becomes hardened to God. Actually, that is an oversimplification of what is transpiring in Pharaoh's heart. In his commentary on Exodus, J. A. Motyer speaks about the "vocabulary of Pharaoh's heart."[1] Motyer's point is that when it comes to Pharaoh's heart and its progressive hardening, we encounter at least three different ways that this process is described. First, Exodus tells us that Pharaoh's heart became hard (Ex. 7:13). Second, Exodus declares that Pharaoh hardened his own heart (Ex. 8:15). Finally, Exodus reveals that the Lord hardened Pharaoh's heart (Ex. 9:12). Motyer notes that all aspects of this vocabulary come to a confluence in Exodus 9:34–10:1:

> When Pharaoh saw that the rain and hail and thun-der had stopped, he sinned again: *He and his officials hardened their hearts*. So *Pharaoh's heart was hard* and he would not let the Israelites go, just as the Lord had said through Moses.
>
> Then the Lord said to Moses, "Go to Pharaoh, for *I have hardened his heart* and the hearts of his officials so that I may perform these signs of mine among them.

Clearly, when it comes to the hardening of Pharaoh's heart there are a variety of influences present, but what does this tell us about both Pharaoh and God in this process?

Motyer suggests that we can tell two stories about the hardening of Pharaoh's heart. The first story has to do with Pharaoh's actions in hardening his own heart. Motyer writes, "One is the story of Pharaoh's moral choices, whereby his heart became increasingly 'set in its ways,' committed more and more irretrievably to a course of geno-cide regarding Israel."[2] The point here is that Pharaoh is responsible for the hardening of his own heart through his own actions and choices. God had revealed himself to Pharaoh and Pharaoh chooses to respond with rebellion. With each rebellion Pharaoh becomes more entrenched in his own wickedness. His heart becomes harder with each sinful choice he makes.

But, as Motyer notes, there is another story to be told as well. Scripture gives us

[a] mere statement that from the perspective of the Lord as moral ruler of his world, the point of no return had been reached and the hardness of Pharaoh's heart must now be judgmentally imposed on him as the justly due consequence of what his own choices had made him.[3]

The story of the hardening of Pharaoh's heart reveals to us that there is a point at which God will no longer abide our rebellion but rightfully judge us for what we are. After repeated rebellions whereby Pharaoh hardened himself against the revelation of God, God judged him for his recalcitrance and sealed his heart of stone.

The story of Pharaoh's heart should not be lost upon us. The dynamics that were at work in his life are not unique to him, even though the redemptive-historical situation in which they occurred was unique. Paul's use of the account of Pharaoh's heart being hardened in Romans 9:14–18 is proof that Pharaoh's case is not unique, but instead reveals general truths about God and his sovereignty over the human heart. God is never complicit in instigating or causing sin, but he is not required to stop us from having what we desire, even if it is sinful.[4] In Romans 1:24, Paul makes this very point when he speaks about God giving over unbelievers, who had continually displayed callousness to sin and rebellion toward God, to their impure and evil desires. This cycle was present in Pharaoh's life. He hardened his hard and then, after his continual rebellion, God hardened his heart and gave Pharaoh over to his desires. But the cycle of hardening that we witness in the account of Pharaoh's heart is not limited to unbelievers.

While a Christian cannot ultimately sin to the point of being lost from the kingdom of God, he or she can become ensnared in a self-hardening cycle whereby the heart becomes calcified toward God. When this happens in our lives, we often bear severe consequences and we build up a tolerance to a particular sin. This portion of the Exodus account reminds us of the interplay between our choices and the sovereignty of God. But it is vital for us to remember that God uses even our sinful choices as a means to ultimately yield new growth in our lives. While recalcitrant unbelievers, like Pharaoh, are often given over to their sinful desires, God never allows his children to spiral relentlessly downward in a maelstrom of their own sinfulness. Through the work of his Spirit and his Word, God convicts us of our sins and softens our hearts, which yields confession and repentance on our part. God's sovereignty extends even over our sinful choices.

THE PLAGUES

The stark contrast between what happened in the hearts of Moses and Pharaoh teaches us about the power and sovereignty of God's will. It reminds us that the great difference between the believer and unbeliever is not the absence of sin, but rather the presence of God's grace in softening, convicting, and renewing the heart of the believer. Ultimately, the difference between Moses and Pharaoh was not that Moses was free of sinful choices, but rather that God chose to have mercy upon Moses. The contrast between Moses and Pharaoh teaches us about the sovereign elective grace of God. But what do the plagues teach us about God? What lesson should we learn from the series of disasters that befell Egypt?

The plagues served many purposes. They were not simply an act of judgment upon Pharaoh and Egypt for rebellion against God and abuse of God's people. They also revealed to Israel that God is powerful and that he is able to save to the uttermost. But the plagues also were not meant for Israel's encouragement alone. Ultimately, the primary purpose of the plagues is to answer Pharaoh's declaration that he did not "know" the God of Israel (Ex. 5:2). Accordingly, throughout the narrative of the plagues God has a constant refrain: "you will know that I am God" (Ex. 7:5, 17; 8:10, 22; 9:14, 16, 29; 10:2). The purpose of the plagues was to convey the knowledge of God, not simply to Egypt or Israel, but to the world.

The plagues fall into a theological category referred to as "signs and wonders." In the Scriptures, when God performs signs and wonders he is generally doing so for a very explicit and twofold purpose.

First, signs and wonders often serve to validate the message of God's messenger or mediator. The plagues served to authenticate the ministry of Moses. They conveyed to Pharaoh and his magicians that Moses was not working on his own authority, but that he was a representative of the Lord. In the New Testament, Jesus used signs and wonders to authenticate his messianic role and confirm his divinity. The Gospel of John, with its seven signs of Jesus, is a great example of the authenticating power of signs and wonders.

A second purpose of signs and wonders is to point beyond themselves to a more significant truth. Yes, the plagues immediately revealed God's power, applied judgment to Egypt, and authenticated Moses' ministry, but they also pointed beyond these immediate events to a greater truth about God's patience. In Exodus 34:6–7, God revealed himself to Moses in a powerful way as

> The LORD, the LORD, the compassionate and gracious God, slow to anger, abounding in love and faithfulness, maintaining love to thousands, and forgiving wickedness, rebellion and sin. Yet he does not leave the guilty unpunished; he punishes the children and their children for the sin of the parents to the third and fourth generation.

These two verses encapsulate the greater meaning of the plagues. God is long-suffering in his application of judgment. He provided Pharaoh and Egypt with ten plagues to spark repentance in them, but they refused to heed the repeated warning. God is patient. In 2 Peter 3:9 we read, "The Lord is not slow in keeping his promise, as some understand slowness. Instead he is patient with you, not wanting anyone to perish, but everyone to come to repentance." The plagues reveal that God is patiently merciful, but they also reveal that there is a point of no return: "he does not leave the guilty unpunished" (Ex. 34:7).

Thus, the plagues served simultaneously to reveal to the world that God is patient in judgment, that he is powerful, and that he can save his people. In these ten plagues is found comforting assurance for those who trust in God and horrific certainty of judgment for those who do not. Some theologians have attempted to say that the type of dynamic revealed in the plagues is reflective of an "Old Testament God" who was judgmental in comparison to the more gracious "New Testament God" revealed in the Gospels and the rest of the New Testament. But in reality, the signs and wonders performed by Jesus, and the very proclamation of the gospel itself, serve a similar ultimate purpose as the plagues. The gospel, like the plagues, serves simultaneously to assure those who trust God of his power to save, and to remind people that, while he is patient, God will ultimately bring judgment upon those who reject his Son and fail to "know the Lord."

THE "WHY" QUESTIONS

But what about the "why" questions such as those we asked at the beginning of this chapter: Why do bad things happen to good people? And why do people do bad things?

These questions lead us to several others: Why did Egypt suffer such awful devastation? Was it because God was unjust? Was it random? Why did "bad things" happen to them? What about the other question? Why did Pharaoh do bad things? Why did he disobey God? Why didn't God change Pharaoh's heart as he did with Moses? Though the Bible does not provide us with detailed answers to these questions, it does clearly reveal that God is just in his actions and sovereign over all things, even human choices and devastating events. Simply put, God is not required to give us answers to these questions. God was also not obligated to transform Pharaoh's heart as he did with Moses; we are not in a position to know why God chose to show mercy on one and not the other. This is not revealed to us and, as his creations, we are in no position to sit in judgment over his decisions. God is not, as C. S. Lewis put it, "in the dock." Ultimately, the answer to these "why" questions is that God will have mercy upon whom he will have mercy (Ex. 33:19; Rom. 9:14–18).

The real question that is so incomprehensible is not one of the two that are so often cited by unbelievers and that we have explored in this chapter. Instead the most bewildering question is: Why does God do good things for bad (sinful) people? The powerful sign that God provided to the world about his patience and long-suffering was not the ten plagues that befell Egypt. Instead, it was the plague of judgment that he poured out on his own Son on the cross. This is an utterly audacious act of grace. Paul recognized the audacity of the cross when he wrote these words in Romans 5:7–8:

> Very rarely will anyone die for a righteous person, though for a good person someone might possibly dare to die. But God demonstrates his own love for us in this: While we were still sinners, Christ died for us.

Sin is the reason that bad things happen in this world and it explains why people rebel against God. Sin answers the two "why" questions that commenced this chapter. But Jesus answers the problem of sin. He is the Lamb of God who takes away the sins of the world (John 1:29).

FOR FURTHER REFLECTION

1. Why do we need to exercise caution in explaining why bad things occur in our world?
2. As Moses confronts Pharaoh, what evidence is there of Moses' spiritual growth? How does Moses' spiritual development mirror that of the apostles? Does his pattern of spiritual development have any corollary in our own lives?
3. What does the hardening of Pharaoh's heart reveal about Pharaoh? What does it reveal about God?
4. In one sense the hardening of Pharaoh's heart was a unique redemptive-historical event, but in another sense it serves to establish a broader paradigm of how God relates to us and how humanity relates to God. How do Romans 1:24 and Romans 9:14–18 serve to support this statement?
5. What purposes did the plagues serve?
6. How does the person and work of Jesus help us to understand the "why" questions discussed in this chapter?

CHAPTER SEVEN

BELIEF, BLOOD, AND BREAD

Exodus 11–12

T here is no doubt that social media websites like Facebook have drastically changed our world and how we relate with one another. Some of these changes have been extremely positive. For instance, these websites allow for rapid communication of news and events among our social groups. This has allowed for swift and coordinated acts of compassion and generosity. One example of this occurred in our local community when Facebook was used to quickly coordinate meals for a family that had a sick child in the hospital. But some of the changes brought by social media websites have not been quite so helpful. For example, they can be used for gossiping, bullying, and simply wasting time. Social media websites are a "double-edged sword."

It is often the case that technological progress and development results in both good and bad consequences. In fact, this dynamic is not limited to the area of technology. It is true of personal, business, and government decisions and policies. The prevalence of this dynamic in our lives explains why we have developed popular idioms like "double-edged sword" or "two sides of the same coin" to describe it with an economy of words. But these idioms also have application to the story of the exodus and the entire unfolding story of redemption.

The Bible is ultimately the account of the application of God's mercy and his judgment. These two acts of God, his mercy and judgment, are often intertwined. They are often like a "double-edged sword" or "two sides of the same coin." For example, when God caused the great flood in Noah's time, he was simultaneously exercising his justice against the world and extending mercy to his covenant people. The most profound example of this dynamic, of course, is the death of Jesus upon the cross. Through the sacrificial death of his Son, God exercised his judgment against our sin while simultaneously granting us mercy.

Of course, there is a major difference between the meaning of these cultural idioms and God's actions. When we employ the cultural idioms of the double-edged sword and two sides of the same coin we are implying that one action results in both positive and negative implications. But when God executes judgment and grants mercy through the same action, both edges of the sword, and both sides of the coin, are equally good and righteous. The exercise of God's judgment and mercy, so often found in the same act, both serve to reveal his power, majesty, and glory.

We see this very same dynamic in God's dealings with the Egyptians, particularly in regard to the plagues pronounced upon them. Every plague suffered by Egypt had a twofold purpose. First, each plague was intended to judge the Egyptians for failing to acknowledge God and for failing to obey his command to let his people go. Second, each plague was intended to display his mercy to Israel by setting them apart from the Egyptians and securing their liberty from their bondage. Both of these aspects of the plagues served to display the glory of God.

In the previous chapter, we witnessed the escalation of God's judgment and mercy as he unleashed the first nine plagues upon Egypt. In this chapter, we will focus solely on the tenth and final plague. While God had judged Egypt in the previous nine plagues, he had also displayed his divine forbearance by allowing time for Egypt to respond, relent, and repent. He even used escalation in the seriousness of the plagues to reinforce the reality of the coming final judgment for disobedience. But the time of divine forbearance had come to an end. It was time for the execution of God's judgment in the form of the death of the firstborn sons of Egypt and for the execution of his mercy to the Israelites in the provision of the Passover.

At first, this chapter of Exodus may sound like a bleak one to read. Certainly, it is a sober chapter in the history of redemption because it involves a most serious judgment of God. But this chapter is not primarily about God's judgment. It is first and foremost an account of God's faithful deliverance of his people through belief, bread, and the blood of the lamb. Here we explore the meaning of the Passover and how it serves as a pattern for the work of redemption secured by the Lord Jesus Christ.

BELIEF

Perhaps you have noticed that as this book has progressed deeper into the story of Moses and the exodus, there seems to be less and less of Moses. In the early chapters of Exodus, and of this book as well, the spotlight was on the life and transformation of Moses. We saw how God turned him from a prideful son in Pharaoh's house to a faithful son in God's house. In the previous chapter, we began to see Moses fade into the background a bit. Yes, he was the human instrument being used by God to announce and deliver the plagues upon Egypt, but it was abundantly clear that the face-off of the plagues was really between God and Pharaoh, not Moses and Pharaoh. This fading of Moses into the background becomes even more pronounced as we explore the final plague wrought upon Egypt. The spotlight is off Moses and decidedly fixed upon God.

Yet, while Moses will progressively fade into the background in this account, he is once again employed as God's mouthpiece to pronounce the plague upon Pharaoh:

> Now the LORD had said to Moses, "I will bring one more plague on Pharaoh and on Egypt. After that, he will let you go from here, and when he does, he will drive you out completely. Tell the people that men and women alike are to ask their neighbors for articles of silver and gold." (Ex. 11:1–2)

At this point, one has to wonder if Moses was feeling a bit frustrated and discouraged. Given what we know about his personality, it seems likely that he was experiencing feelings such as these. After all, he had marched into Pharaoh's presence nine times already, seen God perform miraculous things through him, and yet Pharaoh had not relented. One could even argue that it appeared that Pharaoh was prevailing in his confrontation with God. God had thrown nine plagues Pharaoh's way and yet Pharaoh was still standing firm in his resolve. This must have been frustrating for Moses. Now God was sending Moses to Pharaoh for a tenth time!

But while Moses may have had his doubts about the effectiveness of the plagues, he continued in his faithful obedience to God. Based on God's command, Moses stood before Pharaoh for a tenth time and declared:

> This is what the LORD says: "About midnight I will go throughout Egypt. Every firstborn son in Egypt will die, from the firstborn son of Pharaoh, who sits on the throne, to the firstborn son of the female slave, who is at her hand mill, and all the firstborn of the cattle as well. There will be loud wailing throughout Egypt—worse than there has ever been or ever will be again. But among the Israelites not a dog will bark at any person or animal. Then you will know

that the LORD makes a distinction between Egypt and Israel. All these officials of yours will come to me, bowing down before me and saying, 'Go, you and all the people who follow you!' " After that I will leave. (Ex. 11:4–8)

Moses once again delivered God's message and once again Pharaoh refused to listen. We know about Pharaoh's refusal from the text itself. In Exodus 11:9 we are told that God had revealed to Moses that Pharaoh would not listen: "The LORD had said to Moses, 'Pharaoh will refuse to listen to you so that my wonders may be multiplied in Egypt' "; and in Exodus 11:10 we read, "but the LORD hardened Pharaoh's heart, and he would not let the Israelites go out of his country." We also know that Moses was furious after this tenth meeting with Pharaoh, for Scripture say, "Then Moses, hot with anger, left Pharaoh" (Ex. 11:8).

While Moses had his frustrations, and perhaps some doubts, throughout his interactions with Pharaoh, Moses continued to believe and obey God despite what seemed like a series of triumphs on Pharaoh's part. Moses trusted in the veracity of God's words and he acted upon them. He not only believed God's words at a cognitive level, he also believed them at the volitional level. He heard God's word and he did God's word.

This is one of the themes of the tenth plague and the Passover which was part of it. The final plague and the Passover set before us many stark contrasts. There is the contrast between judgment and deliverance. There is also the contrast between belief and unbelief. Moses believed what God said and did it, but Pharaoh rejected God's word and ignored it. But Moses was not the only example of belief in the account of the tenth plague; the entire nation of Israel displayed remarkable faithfulness in their response to God's word.

After God explained to Moses what would occur in the tenth plague and what the people of Israel must do to avoid this judgment impacting them, he sent Moses to convey his instructions and expectations to Israel. Moses was sent as the mediator of God's message. Like a modern preacher, Moses was called to proclaim to Israel the pathway of salvation from God's judgment. Moses immediately obeyed God, and he summoned all the elders of Israel to instruct them regarding God's commands:

> Go at once and select the animals for your families and slaughter the Passover lamb. Take a bunch of hyssop, dip it into the blood in the basin and put some of the blood on the top and on both sides of the doorframe. None of you shall go out of the door of your house until morning. When the LORD goes through the land to strike down the Egyptians, he will see the blood on the top and sides of the doorframe and will pass over that doorway, and he will not permit the destroyer to enter your houses and strike you down. (Ex. 12:21–23)

After Moses explained God's instructions to avoid the judgment of the tenth plague, he then issued a command to obey God's instructions: "Obey these instructions as a lasting ordinance for you and your descendants" (Ex. 12:24). But the question arises, how did Israel respond to this command to obey God?

If you know anything about the Old Testament and the history of Israel, you know that the nation of Israel often failed in its calling to be a light to the nations. The Scriptures display that God's chosen people often chose to disobey his word and to do what was right in their own eyes. The Old Testament book of Judges is perhaps the most poignant example of this cycle of disobedience on the part of Israel. But in this instance in Exodus, Israel displayed remarkable faithfulness. After Moses commanded obedience, Israel rendered obedience. The first reaction of Israel was to bow down and worship the Lord (Ex. 12:27). This act of worship is followed by an unequivocal declaration of the Israelites' complete obedience to God's word: "The Israelites did just what the LORD commanded Moses and Aaron" (Ex. 12:28). Like Moses, Israel heard God's word and they did God's word.

One of the lessons of the Passover is the vital importance of rendering obedience to God's word. God provided the means for Israel's salvation from the judgment of the tenth plague, but he commanded them to respond by embracing and believing this means of salvation. But even Israel's act of belief was a gift of God. We know this because of the example of Pharaoh as discussed in the previous chapter. God is sovereign over the heart and over the extension of his mercy and judgment. Moses' and Israel's belief was commendable, but it must be considered as a gift of God. The apostle Paul makes this clear in the New Testament when he speaks of the faith that believers exercise in accepting the truth of the gospel, "For it is by grace you have been saved, through faith—and this is not from yourselves, it is the gift of God—not by works, so that no one can boast" (Eph. 2:8–9). This statement is equally applicable to the Israelites and their being saved from the judgment of the tenth plague. Moses and Israel exercised faith, but that faith was a gift of God.

The Passover is clearly a type of the work of Jesus Christ in delivering his chosen people from the judgment of God's wrath. The Passover foreshadows the proclamation of the gospel. The Passover event also makes clear that salvation requires belief and faith in the message of God. Israel got this right and they were saved from the judgment of God. The same demand for belief is set upon every heart as the gospel of Jesus Christ is proclaimed and salvation is only granted to those who, by the gift of faith, embrace and believe it: "Believe in the Lord Jesus, and you will be saved—you and your household" (Acts 16:31).

BLOOD

While faith and belief served as the instrument through which Israel gained access to God's provided means of salvation, that salvation also required another element—the shedding and application of the blood of the lamb. God provided the following instructions to Moses regarding this second element of his plan of salvation:

> Tell the whole community of Israel that on the tenth day of this month each man is to take a lamb for his family, one for each household. If any household is too small for a whole lamb, they must share one with their nearest neighbor, having taken into account the number of people there are. You are to determine the amount of lamb needed in accordance with what each person will eat. The animals you choose must be year-old males without defect, and you may take them from the sheep or the goats. Take care of them until the fourteenth day of the month, when all the members of the community of Israel must slaughter them at twilight. Then they are to take some of the blood and put it on the sides and tops of the doorframes of the houses where they eat the lambs. (Ex. 12:3–7)

Israel's salvation from the tenth plague was to be sealed with the blood of a lamb. Each and every household was required to shed blood and apply it to the doorframe of their respective homes. While the blood of the lamb served numerous instructive purposes in teaching Israel about how God secures the salvation of his people, the two most significant functions of the blood revealed in the Passover account are that it served as a sign and as a substitute.

The Blood of the Lamb as a Sign

All of the plagues that God sent upon the nation of Egypt served to distinguish between Israel and Egypt. The judgment of God was not meant for his people. But it is particularly in the last plague that we see God commanding a demonstrative act on Israel's part to demarcate itself from the Egyptians. Israel was told to use the blood of the lamb as a physical and visible sign of its distinction from the Egyptians. Each household of Israel had to physically apply the sign to the doorframe of their respective homes in order to benefit from God's mercy:

> Then Moses summoned all the elders of Israel and said to them, "Go at once and select the animals for your families and slaughter the Passover lamb. Take a bunch of hyssop, dip it into the blood in the basin and put some of the blood on the top and on both sides of the doorframe. None of you shall go out of the door of your house until morning. When the LORD goes through the land to strike down the Egyptians, he will see the blood on the top and sides of the doorframe and will pass over that doorway, and he will not permit the destroyer to enter your houses and strike you down. (Ex. 12:21–23)

It was the physical presence of this sign upon the top and sides of the doorframe, as seen by the Lord, which yielded protection, safety, and salvation to the Israelites.

The blood of the lamb was a physical sign that sealed the salvation of Israel from the judgment of the death of the firstborn. God often uses physical signs as seals of his promises to save his people from wrath. Circumcision served as such a sign in the old covenant economy. In the New Testament, the waters of baptism and the tangible symbolism of the elements of the Lord's Table serve similar functions. The Passover reminds us of the significance of the act of demarcating ourselves as being of the Lord through the means of grace that he has provided to us. One can't help but compare the household application of the blood of the lamb to the household baptisms of the New

Testament. Consider, for example, the household baptism that occurred in the house of the Philippian jailer:

> They replied, "Believe in the Lord Jesus, and you will be saved—you and your household." Then they spoke the word of the Lord to him and to all the others in his house. At that hour of the night the jailer took them and washed their wounds; then immediately he and all his household were baptized. (Acts 16:31–33)

As in the Passover, the household of the Philippian jailer believed God and applied the sign of his salvation. The Passover reminds us of the importance of the application of the signs and seals of God's covenant with us. It particularly reminds us of the work of Jesus Christ in protecting us from the wrath of God because the blood of the lamb was not only a sign, it was also a substitute.

The Blood of the Lamb as a Substitute

Something was required to die on the night of the Passover. Death and the shedding of blood were required. The options for the Israelites were their firstborn sons or the blood of the lamb, but the fact that blood was required was not up for debate. By requiring a substituted sacrifice for their firstborn sons, God was teaching his people the concept of substitutionary atonement. This act of substitution, of course, foreshadows the work of Jesus in the New Testament. In fact, the connection is made explicit by John the Baptist, who, upon first seeing Jesus declared, "Look, the Lamb of God, who takes away the sin of the world!" (John 1:29).

There are other parallels between Jesus and the Passover lamb. First, the Israelites were commanded to choose a perfect lamb for their substitute; the lamb was required to be "without defect" (Ex. 12:5). Jesus had no defect. He was perfect in every way, as the writer to the Hebrews reminds us: "For we do not have a high priest who is unable to empathize with our weaknesses, but we have one who has been tempted in every way, just as we are—yet he did not sin" (Heb. 4:15). The apostle Peter makes the connection even more explicitly:

> For you know that it was not with perishable things such as silver or gold that you were redeemed from the empty way of life handed down to you from your ancestors, but with the precious blood of Christ, a lamb without blemish or defect. (1 Peter 1:18–19)

Jesus Is the Perfect Passover Lamb

Another parallel between the sacrifice of the Passover lamb and the sacrifice which Jesus made is the sufficiency of the act. The Passover event was a unique, one-time, redemptive-historical event. While the Passover event was to be remembered and celebrated annually, the actual historical event and the redemption it secured were unique. The sacrifice which Jesus made is a similar one-time event. While we remember the death and sacrifice of Jesus every time we celebrate the Lord's Supper, his actual death and sacrifice, and the redemption they secured, were unique, one-time events. The writer to the Hebrews reminds us of the unique, once-for-all sufficiency of the work of Jesus our Great High Priest: "But when this priest had offered for all time one sacrifice for sins, he sat down at the right hand of God" (Heb. 10:12).

The Passover event, particularly the sacrifice of the lamb and the application of its blood, is a powerful Old Testament proclamation of the forthcoming work of Jesus Christ. One cannot really overstate the explicit foreshadowing of the Passover to the work of Jesus. In fact, the connection is so overwhelming and the nexus so tight that Paul refers to Jesus as "our Passover lamb" (1 Cor. 5:7). Like Israel, we are all saved by the sign and substitute of the blood of the Lamb. As the apostle John reminds us in Revelation 12:11, the triumph of the church, its victory over the dragon, was secured "by the blood of the Lamb."

BREAD

Although the Passover was a unique redemptive-historical event, God did not want Israel to ever forget it and its meaning. He commanded the Israelites to remember this event through an annual celebration:

> This is a day you are to commemorate; for the generations to come you shall celebrate it as a festival to the LORD—a lasting ordinance. For seven days you are to eat bread made without yeast. On the first day remove the yeast from your houses, for whoever eats anything with yeast in it from the first day through the seventh must be cut off from Israel. (Ex. 12:14–15)

Israel was called upon to commemorate the Passover for generations. It was to be a "lasting ordinance" and a "festival to the LORD" (Ex. 12:14). God also explained the reason why the Passover should be commemorated for generations: "Celebrate the Festival of Unleavened Bread, because it was on this very day that I brought your divisions out of Egypt. Celebrate this day as a lasting ordinance for the generations to come" (Ex. 12:17). The reason the Passover was to be remembered was because it marked the commencement of the exodus from Egypt. The Passover marked the beginning of Israel's liberation from bondage.

Remembrance is an important part of our faith. God wanted Israel to never forget the work of redemption that he had wrought on their behalf. He instructed them to observe the ceremony even after they entered the land God had promised to them (Ex. 12:25). God even instructed them to instruct their children regarding the reason for this time of remembrance:

> And when your children ask you, "What does this ceremony mean to you?" then tell them, "It is the Passover sacrifice to the LORD, who passed over the houses of the Israelites in Egypt and spared our homes when he struck down the Egyptians." Then the people bowed down and worshiped. (Ex. 12:26–27)

Israel was called to remember their redemption from Egypt.

In the New Testament, we see a similar call to remember our redemption. Jesus celebrated what became the Lord's Supper during the Passover feast. This Last Supper not only foreshadowed his imminent work of redemption on the cross, but it also demarcated a transition from the old to the new covenant. The Passover Feast, which required remembrance of the exodus, was now giving way to its fulfillment in the exodus realized through the cross of Jesus Christ. During the Last Supper, Jesus made a new covenant in his blood, the blood of the Lamb. He also instituted a feast to remember his soon-to-be-completed work on the cross. As Paul notes in 1 Corinthians 11:25–26, as he passes on the ordinance that Christ gave to him:

> In the same way, after supper he took the cup, saying, "This cup is the new covenant in my blood; do this, whenever you drink it, in remembrance of me." For whenever you eat this bread and drink this cup, you proclaim the Lord's death until he comes.

Like the Israelites, we are to remember perpetually our exodus from bondage to sin, Satan, and death by celebrating with a meal.

We have already seen that the Passover involved the shedding and application of the blood of the lamb, but there was another tangible element that was part of the Passover celebration—the eating of unleavened bread. Why the bread? Why unleavened bread? What did this particular food have to do with God's redemption of his people from Egypt? There were some simple practical reasons why the bread was unleavened, as is revealed by Exodus 12:39: "The dough was without yeast because they had been driven out of Egypt and did not have time to prepare food for themselves." But there is more significance to the centrality of the unleavened bread to the celebration of the Passover.

In 1 Corinthians 5:7–8, the apostle Paul looks back to the Passover and applies its significance to the life of the new covenant church. Note how he uses the imagery of the unleavened bread:

> Get rid of the old yeast, so that you may be a new unleavened batch—as you really are. For Christ, our Passover lamb, has been sacrificed. Therefore let us keep the Festival, not with the old bread leavened with malice and wickedness, but with the unleavened bread of sincerity and truth.

For us to fully understand Paul's point here we need to understand a bit more about leaven. Leaven is created by taking a small portion of existing dough and allowing it to ferment. The leaven is then added to a new batch of dough, which allows the bread to rise. But there is a risk in continuing to use the same leaven. Leaven could become infected or tainted, thereby leading to the spoiling of the new dough and the entire loaf of bread. Accordingly, it is important for health reasons to get rid of the old leaven and to create a new batch. But Paul is not primarily giving health advice in these verses; instead he is using leaven in a spiritual and metaphorical sense. He is calling the church to respond to the death of Christ by removing the old leaven of our sinful lives and replacing it with the unleavened bread of our new lives in Christ. In other words, Paul is calling the church to live in light of the redemption secured by the once-for-all sacrifice of Christ the Passover lamb.

With Paul's words from 1 Corinthians in mind, we see that the unleavened bread served as a metaphor in the life of Israel. It was a stark reminder to them that, because of God's work of redemption, they were no longer in bondage to Egypt. With this new freedom came a new responsibility. They were not to carry with them the leaven of Egypt. It was time for them to separate themselves entirely from that prior bondage, both physically and spiritually. They were to leave Egypt in every way.

As we have already seen from Paul's use of the unleavened bread imagery in 1 Corinthians 5:7-8, this principle continues to apply to the church today. When we embrace Christ as our Passover, we must change our lives. We must leave behind the old and embrace the new. As Paul states in 2 Corinthians 5:17, "Therefore, if anyone is in Christ, the new creation has come: The old has gone, the new is here!"

Although the Lord's Supper does not have to be celebrated with unleavened bread, the parallels between the Passover and this celebration meal of the new covenant should not be lost upon us. At the table of the Lord we eat and drink because he instituted the ordinance and we do it in remembrance of the one who led us out of bondage. Our response to such a great redemptive act is to live in gratitude to the one who redeemed us by casting out the old leaven and living for him in sincerity and truth.

CHRIST OUR PASSOVER

As I mentioned earlier in this chapter, there is not much of Moses in the account of the Passover. The focus here is on God's judgment upon the Egyptians and his mercy upon the Israelites. God draws a stark line of demarcation between Egypt and Israel. Redemption is afforded to those who believe in God's appointed means of salvation, embrace and apply the blood of the lamb, and eat the bread of their new life in remembrance of what God has done for them.

As the pages of Scripture turn to the new covenant and the coming of the one who is the true Lamb of God and who is Christ our Passover, we see all of these shadows embracing their fulfillment. The purpose of the Passover is realized in Christ.

FOR FURTHER REFLECTION

1. Why does the focus of the book of Exodus slowly move away from Moses to God when it comes to the plagues, particularly the tenth plague?
2. How did Israel evidence its faithfulness in response to the pronouncement of the tenth plague?
3. What two purposes did the blood of the lamb serve during the Passover?
4. What purposes did the bread serve in the Passover? Why was it unleavened?
5. How does the Passover foreshadow the person and work of Jesus Christ?

CHAPTER EIGHT

TAKING THE HARD ROAD

Exodus 13–19

I remember well the day that I learned that I passed the bar examination. I had taken the two-day exam in July and did not learn that I passed until the middle of December. I can remember praying over that envelope as I tore it open. When I saw that I had passed I rejoiced. I thought to myself, "Finally, now the hard part is over!" Boy, was I wrong. I soon began working for a large law firm and felt the pressures and demands of meeting my goals for billable hours. The work had just begun. It was a hard road.

Perhaps you have had similar experiences in your life. You achieve some long sought after goal, have an amazing triumph, and then you are rudely awakened by the reality of the difficult road ahead. Often our celebrations end quickly in the light of the reality that the hardest part is not behind us, but rather ahead of us. Have you ever had an experience like that? It can be very frustrating to come off the joy of a great victory only to encounter another, perhaps more difficult, challenge.

I think it is fair to say that Moses and the Israelites must have experienced something similar to this dynamic after the victory of the Passover and the ensuing exodus from Egypt. Moses had watched as God sent plague upon plague on Egypt.

He had seen God's commands turn into fulfillment. He had witnessed the carnage that befell Egypt, culminating in the death of Egypt's firstborn sons. He had watched God bring Pharaoh to his knees and heard Pharaoh relent. God had won the victory and Israel had been freed from its bondage.

But Israel's battles were far from over. The road ahead of them was fraught with new perils as well as old enemies. Hidden in the midst of this great victory was the seed of a future battle. A greater test remained for Israel, and this time the proctor of the exam was God:

> When Pharaoh let the people go, God did not lead them on the road through the Philistine country, though that was shorter. For God said, "If they face war, they might change their minds and return to Egypt." So God led the people around by the desert road toward the Red Sea. The Israelites went up out of Egypt ready for battle. (Ex. 13:17–18)

Israel was not to take the direct route to the land of promise. They were, by God's decree, to take the long road through the desert. While this circuitous route may have first seemed like a way to avoid conflict, since after all they were bypassing the country presently inhabited by the ancestors of the people who would later become known as the Philistines, in the end it would force them to confront an even greater enemy than the Egyptians or the ancestors of the Philistines. That enemy was themselves. Israel's struggles were far from over. They were about to battle with their own self-love and the human desire for autonomy. They were headed to the desert. God told them to take the hard road.

THE HARD ROAD

Chapters 14–19 of Exodus chronicle a series of challenges that the Israelites faced on their journey to the land that God had promised to them. The challenges spanned the spectrum from military struggle to hunger and thirst. Each victory quickly yielded to a new battle. This series of struggles tested Israel's resolve. It was so trying that Israel frequently yearned to return to the slavery of Egypt instead of going on with the fight. They often voiced their harsh displeasure with their circumstances to their leader, Moses. Moses was about to experience his second trial in a desert land, this time as the leader of a contemptuous people. But God is not arbitrary. He had a purpose in leading his people down this hard road. But before we get to the reason for the hard road, let's travel that road with Moses and Israel and experience it with them. The hardships began on the banks of the Red Sea.

THE BATTLE AT THE RED SEA

The problems for Israel began almost immediately after escaping Egypt. They had just been released from the clutches of Pharaoh and now God told Moses to turn around and wait for Egypt's pursuing armies (Ex. 14:1–4). After letting Israel go, Pharaoh quickly repented of his actions as it dawned upon him that he was losing his free labor force (Ex. 14:5). So Pharaoh responded by summoning his military might to pursue the Israelites.

When the Israelites saw Pharaoh's army charging toward them they were terrified. They rushed to Moses and lodged their complaints:

Was it because there were no graves in Egypt that you brought us to the desert to die? What have you done to us by bringing us out of Egypt? Didn't we say to you in Egypt, "Leave us alone; let us serve the Egyptians"? It would have been better for us to serve the Egyptians than to die in the desert! (Ex. 14:11–12)

103

This would not be the last time that Moses would hear this type of complaint. One might think that Moses' response to them would contain a certain level of indignation regarding their faithlessness and ingratitude, but Moses was now a different man than he was in his early days. He was more patient and long-suffering. He was more like his Lord. Moses answered the people by assuring them, "Do not be afraid. Stand firm and you will see the deliverance the LORD will bring you today. The Egyptians you see today you will never see again. The LORD will fight for you; you need only to be still" (Ex. 14:13–14).

Israel's back was against the wall. In front of them was the angered mob of the Egyptian army and at their backs was the seemingly unpassable Red Sea. But then God instructed Moses to raise his staff and to stretch out his hand over the sea in order to divide the water (Ex. 14:16). Moses did as he was told and the waters divided, allowing Israel to safely pass through to the other side. Pharaoh and his men were not so fortunate. God commanded Moses to close the passageway through the water so that the walls of water would collapse upon the Egyptian army as it attempted to cross the Red Sea. The end result was the utter destruction of Pharaoh and his army. God had won a complete victory and the Israelites witnessed the mighty outstretched arm of God. The account ends with these words:

> That day the LORD saved Israel from the hands of the Egyptians, and Israel saw the Egyptians lying dead on the shore. And when the Israelites saw the mighty hand of the LORD displayed against the Egyptians, the people feared the LORD and put their trust in him and in Moses his servant. (Ex. 14:30–31)

God had once again delivered his people from their enemies, and Israel proclaimed a newfound trust in God and in Moses his servant. But the hardships for Israel were just beginning. The road to the land of promise was not only hard, it was long as well.

THE DESERT OF SHUR

After their incredible victory at the Red Sea, Israel entered a time of jubilation. The Red Sea victory was so definitive and the nation of Israel was filled with assurance regarding God's plan for them. This assurance was made evident through the composition and singing of a song. Exodus 15:1–18 contains the inspired lyrics to this anthem of praise to God. It was song by Moses and the entire nation of Israel. The content of the song stresses both the past victory at the Red Sea and the future hope of the nation of Israel. For example, the song contains this reflection upon the Red Sea victory: "The LORD is a warrior; the LORD is his name. Pharaoh's chariots and his army he has hurled into the sea" (Ex. 15:3–4). The song also contains this declaration of Israel's confidence regarding the future:

The nations will hear and tremble;
    anguish will grip the people of Philistia.
The chiefs of Edom will be terrified,
    the leaders of Moab will be seized with trembling,
the people of Canaan will melt away;
    terror and dread will fall on them.
By the power of your arm
    they will be as still as a stone—
until your people pass by, LORD,
    until the people you bought pass by.
You will bring them in and plant them
    on the mountain of your inheritance—
the place, LORD, you made for your dwelling,
    the sanctuary, LORD, your hands established.
The LORD reigns for ever and ever. (Ex. 15:14–18)

But this moment of national celebration would soon fade in the memories of the Israelites. They would soon fall from this peak and return to the hard road. After this time of celebration Moses led the Israelites away from the banks of the Red Sea and into the Desert of Shur (Ex. 15:22).

Israel was back in the harshness of the desert. Water was extremely hard to find. They were getting thirsty. It took them all of three days to forget God's faithfulness to them at the Red Sea. They arrived at a place called Marah, where they actually found water, but it was bitter and undrinkable (Ex. 15:23). Then the people lodged their formal complaint with Moses, "So the people grumbled against Moses, saying, 'What are we to drink?'" (Ex. 15:24).

Moses responded by seeking the Lord and the Lord showed him a piece of wood and instructed him to throw it in the water (Ex. 15:25). Moses obeyed and the bitter water of Marah became drinkable. After that they arrived at Elim, where they encountered twelve springs of fresh drinkable water, and they made their camp there (Ex. 15:27). God had once again delivered his people from danger.

THE DESERT OF SIN

After enjoying the oasis of Elim, the Israelites moved on to another stop on the hardship highway. They entered yet another desert, the desert of Sin. Whereas the previous desert was short on water, this new desert was lacking food. As the bellies of the Israelites began to grumble, so too did their mouths. The complaints once again came to Moses:

In the desert the whole community grumbled against Moses and Aaron. The Israelites said to them, "If only we had died by the LORD's hand in Egypt! There we sat around pots of meat and ate all the food we wanted, but you have brought us out into this desert to starve this entire assembly to death." (Ex. 16:2–3)

Once again Israel revealed a heart of faithlessness and ingratitude. The song of victory at the banks of the Red Sea had fully faded from their memory and from their lips. They were no longer exalting God and trusting in Moses; they were bitterly complaining against God and ready to rebel against Moses.

But once again God met the needs of his people. He delivered them from their hunger by giving them meat to eat in the evening and bread to eat in the morning (Ex. 16:4–8). Each evening the skies rained quail and each morning the ground was rife with manna. The manna would come to represent the entire wilderness wanderings of the Israelites. They would eat it for forty years, until they reached the borders of the land of promise (Ex. 16:35). God once again provided for his people.

THE DESERT OF REPHIDIM

After leaving the desert of Sin, the Israelites next camped at the city of Rephidim. Like their experience in the desert of Shur, Rephidim was a place without water. Israel was once again suffering from thirst, and they made their displeasure known to Moses: "So they quarreled with Moses and said, 'Give us water to drink' " (Ex. 17:2).

Moses must have been growing a bit tired of this cycle. After all the dangers, toils, and snares through which God had brought his people, Moses must have chafed to see them constantly lacking faith and distrusting in his leadership and God's provision for them. You can see a bit of Moses' frustration in how he replied to the Israelites' demand for water: "Moses replied, 'Why do you quarrel with me? Why do you put the LORD to the test?' " (Ex. 17:2). But the people did not relent. They snapped back at Moses, "Why did you bring us up out of Egypt to make us and our children and livestock die of thirst?" (Ex. 17:3). Moses was miffed and even a bit afraid. The crowds were angered and restless.

Moses did the only thing he could do. He sought God for help. "Then Moses cried out to the Lord, 'What am I to do with these people? They are almost ready to stone me'" (Ex. 17:4). God answered Moses' concerns and the needs of his people by instructing Moses to strike a rock with his staff. Upon his striking the rock, water flowed from it to quench the parching thirst of the Israelites (Ex. 17:5–6). But Moses was getting a bit fed up with the behavior of the Israelites, and he named the location where this occurred Massah (which means "testing") and Meribah (which means "quarreling") "because the Israelites quarreled and because they tested the LORD saying, 'Is the LORD among us or not?'" (Ex. 17:7). The pattern here is the same, Israel grumbled and God provided.

THE AMALEKITES

Israel's trials at Rephidim were not over. After quenching their thirst with the water from the rock, the Israelites were confronted by another military challenge. The Amalekites came and attacked them (Ex. 17:8). First it was the Egyptian army, now they were being pursued by the Amalekite army. Israel was facing one trial after another.

Israel prevailed in their conflict with the Amalekites. Moses went to the top of a hill and, as long as his hands were held up, the Israelites gained the upper hand in the battle. Aaron and Hur helped to keep Moses' arms up until the victory was won (Ex. 17:10–12). Moses built an altar there and worshipped the Lord. He called the place "The LORD is my Banner" (Ex. 17:15). Moses, and the Israelites, had once again been delivered by their Lord.

ARRIVING AT SINAI

After all of these trials, Israel would eventually arrive at yet another desert. "On the first day of the third month after the Israelites left Egypt—on that very day—they came to the Desert of Sinai" (Ex. 19:1). Some extraordinary things would happen there, but that is for the next chapter. At this point it is important to pause and reflect on God's purpose in sending Israel down this hard road. Why did God follow the redemption event of the exodus with such a series of trials—and eventually forty years of wilderness wandering? Why did he take them on a desert road? What are we to learn from this account?

A PEOPLE IN THE WILDERNESS

There is no doubt that God was the one who led Israel on its path through the wilderness. As we can see from Exodus 13:17, God was concerned to take the Israelites directly into the jaws of the mighty Philistines: "When Pharaoh let the people go, God did not lead them on the road through the Philistine country, though that was shorter. For God said, 'If they face war, they might change their minds and return to Egypt.'" So God instead chose the longer wilderness route to take his people to the land of promise.

But there was more to God's purposes in choosing this path than simply avoiding the Philistine army. After all, God was their warrior and he could easily have vanquished the Philistines or any other army for that matter. God had something more in mind in choosing the hard road for his people. Israel had to learn that the pathway to the land of promise is difficult and that they would only get there if they relied upon the strength of the Lord rather than on their own strength.

Though it may seem that Israel was constantly putting God to the test, it was actually God who was putting Israel to the test. He was teaching his people something about themselves. He was showing them how much they needed him to survive, and he was showing them that he was sufficient to provide for them. He was demonstrating to them that he, and only he, could bring them to the land of promise.

The forty years in the wilderness was God's way of wringing Israel's self-love and self-sufficiency out of his people, much as he had done with their leader, Moses. Remember, Moses spent forty years in a desert wasteland being transformed from a prideful fugitive to God's servant. What died in the deserts of Shur, Sin, Rephidim, and Sinai was Israel's sense that they could go it alone. They also learned that life after redemption was not meant to be easy. It is a hard road to the land of promise.

Of course, the wilderness wanderings of Israel were not only real historical events, but they also have metaphorical and spiritual meaning that relates to the universal experience of all believers. The wilderness wanderings of Israel reveal a template of the pilgrim life of Christians. After our redemption by the work of Christ, we enter into a period of wilderness wandering as we long to arrive at the land of promise. The land of promise for us is not the physical land of Canaan, but rather that land of rest to which Adam looked forward. Our land of promise is an eternity with Christ unencumbered by the remaining sinful desires we have as believers in the wilderness of this age.

The entire book of Hebrews is arguably based on the idea that the Christian life mirrors that of the wilderness wanderings of Israel. The original recipients of that epistle were under great persecution and were wondering if they should turn back to their former way of life, much like the Israelites wondered if they would have been better off back in Egypt. In fact, the writer of Hebrews uses the unbelief of the generation of Israel which died in the wilderness due to its lack of trust in God as a warning to these early Christians:

> Who were they who heard and rebelled? Were they not all those Moses led out of Egypt? And with whom was he angry for forty years? Was it not with those

who sinned, whose bodies perished in the wilderness? And to whom did God swear that they would never enter his rest if not to those who disobeyed? So we see that they were not able to enter, because of their unbelief. (Heb. 3:16–19)

But the writer to the Hebrews did not leave his hearers in despair. While calling them away from the example of that unfaithful generation, he also called these early Christians to place their faith in Jesus. He spurred them on, not by telling them that suffering would cease, but by assuring them that Jesus would bring them to the land of promise. Think of Hebrews 12:1–3, where the writer to the Hebrews declares:

Therefore, since we are surrounded by such a great cloud of witnesses, let us throw off everything that hinders and the sin that so easily entangles. And let us run with perseverance the race marked out for us, fixing our eyes on Jesus, the pioneer and perfecter of faith. For the joy set before him he endured the cross, scorning its shame, and sat down at the right hand of the throne of God. Consider him who endured such opposition from sinners, so that you will not grow weary and lose heart.

The call is to persevere through the trials of this age and to place our trust in Jesus Christ. This is exactly what God was teaching Israel in the wilderness.

The sufferings of this life are never denied by the Scriptures. Redemption in Christ is not followed by a primrose path. Instead, Jesus calls us to the hardest task of all: "Whoever wants to be my disciple must deny themselves and take up their cross daily and follow me" (Luke 9:23). Jesus calls us to enter the wilderness, just as he himself did in his encounter with Satan, and to trust in him and every word that comes from the mouth of God. This is what

God was teaching Israel on the hard road of the wilderness, and this is what he is still teaching us today.

THE GOD WHO PROVIDES

But the story of the hard road is not ultimately a story of trials, tribulations, and failures. Yes, it reveals the frailty of the human heart and how soon we lose our faith and trust in God. But the wilderness account of Israel is ultimately about triumph and victory—God's triumph and his victory.

Each and every struggle that Israel encountered on that road was met by the love and provision of God. When their backs were against the wall at the Red Sea, God provided the military victory over the Egyptians. When they were thirsty in the desert of Shur, God turned the bitter waters sweet and gave them the oasis of Elim. When they were hungry in the desert of Sin, God provided them with meat and bread. When thirst came again at Rephidim, God provided again with water from a rock. Finally, when the Amalekites waged war against them, God emerged as their mighty warrior once again and crushed the foes of Israel.

The most important lesson of the wilderness wanderings is not that we are incapable and insufficient in ourselves, which is certainly true; rather, the lesson is that God is stronger than any enemy we face in this life. He is the God who provides for his people and his salvation will not fail. He will bring his people home. That is the story of the wilderness. God brings his people home.

The same is true for believers today. God will leave none of his people behind and no enemy will triumph over his love. As Jesus put it, "I give them eternal life, and they shall never perish; no one will snatch them out of my hand" (John 10:28). The hard road is real, but it ends with rest. It ends at the land of promise—and Jesus promises to bring us there.

FOR FURTHER REFLECTION

1. This chapter focused on the arduous journey of the Israelites in the wilderness after their miraculous victory at the Red Sea. Have you ever experienced the discouragement of achieving some great success only to face a new and greater challenge? How did this impact your spiritual life?

2. What were the names of the three deserts through which the Israelites journeyed? What happened to them when they travelled through each of these deserts?

3. What were God's purposes in taking Israel on the "hard road" through the wilderness?

4. What does Israel's "hard road" journey teach us about our spiritual journey as New Testament believers?

5. What is the ultimate lesson of the wilderness wanderings of Israel? What did it teach them and what should it teach us?

CHAPTER NINE

THE LAW CAME
THROUGH MOSES

Exodus 19–30

T
he wilderness wanderings of Israel were not easy times for Moses. His leadership was constantly challenged. Every complaint and problem that arose in this burgeoning nation came to him. He heard all the grumbling and complaining. By the time Israel reached Mount Sinai, Moses must have been exhausted and frustrated. Perhaps Moses was also feeling a bit despondent himself over where things were going. He must have been wondering if they would ever get to the land of promise. He must have questioned if God knew what he was doing. After all, the people had been wandering around in the desert for quite some time. Moses and his people were in need of some reassurance regarding God's love for them. They received that assurance at Mount Sinai.

At Mount Sinai, Israel received the heart of the old covenant and Moses reached the pinnacle of his mediatorial work. At Mount Sinai, God cemented his covenant relationship with this nascent nation that he had elected from all the nations of the earth to be his firstborn son (Ex. 4:22). It was at Mount Sinai that God shared with his children how they were to serve him. He taught them how to live and how to worship him. There he gave Moses and the people a definitive and distilled declaration of his moral law in the Ten Commandments; he also provided instructions regarding how he should be worshipped by giving Moses the plans for the tabernacle. In this chapter, we will focus upon this twofold instruction that God gave to his people through his servant Moses.

THE PROLOGUE TO THE GIVING
OF THE LAW

Often we as Christians take the Ten Commandments out of their original context. This is very easy to do because we so often encounter the Commandments as excerpted material in our church bulletins or on a plaque on the wall. While the Ten Commandments are representative of the timeless standards of God's moral law, we nevertheless increase the risk of misinterpreting them when we strip them from their covenantal and redemptive-historical context.

We have already noted that the law was shared with Moses and Israel at a time when they were fatigued from their wilderness wanderings. They were betwixt the great victory of the Red Sea and the borders of the land of promise. They wanted to enter the land that God had promised them, but they were not ready. God had not finished his preparatory work. The people of Israel needed to understand what it meant to live in covenant with the God who had brought them out of Egypt. They needed to understand God's love and his expectations. This is the context in which the law was given. It was given to immature believers who had to learn how to respond to God's grace and to live a life pleasing to him.

In Exodus 19, we see that God sets the stage for the giving of the law by establishing the nature of his relationship with his people. God also uses this opportunity to reaffirm his relationship with Moses and to confirm Moses' unique role as mediator. In Exodus 19, Moses ascends the mountain three times to enter into the presence of God, and each time descends to share God's words with the people. This series of ascents and descents accomplishes several things. First, it affirms the holiness of God. God, while near to his people, must also be separate from them because of his holiness. Second, it confirms that Moses is God's undisputed mediator. God does not speak to Israel directly, but he mediates his message through Moses. Third, this series of ascents and descents, along with the communication that followed, serve to reassure Moses and the people that God is with them and loves them.

THE FIRST ASCENT

The first ascent of Moses is documented in Exodus 19:3–6. Moses ascended the mountain and God told him what to say to Israel:

> Then Moses went up to God, and the LORD called to him from the mountain and said, "This is what you are to say to the descendants of Jacob and what you are to tell the people of Israel: 'You yourselves have seen what I did to Egypt, and how I carried you on eagles' wings and brought you to myself. Now if you obey me fully and keep my covenant, then out of all nations you will be my treasured possession. Although the whole earth is mine, you will be for me a kingdom of priests and a holy nation.' These are the words you are to speak to the Israelites." (Ex. 19:3–6)

In God's first communication with Moses at Sinai he set forth some basic building blocks of his relationship with Israel. He was providing context for his covenant and law.

117

First, God begins his discourse by setting everything within the context of his redemptive deliverance of the people from their bondage in Egypt: "You yourselves have seen what I did to Egypt, and how I carried you on eagles' wings and brought you to myself" (Ex. 19:4). God had purchased, or redeemed, Israel and it was this act that set them apart under his covenantal love. Israel had done nothing to earn that redemption from Egypt and they did not contribute to it. It was a unilateral act of God's unconditional love.

While God's redemption of Israel was unconditional and unilateral, this redemption had created a relationship between God and Israel, and God had clear expectations regarding how his people should respond to that act of deliverance. God expected his people to live according to his laws. He expected them to obey him: "Now if you obey me fully and keep my covenant, then out of all nations you will be my treasured possession" (Ex. 19:5).

Finally, God revealed to Israel both the extent of his kingship and the depth of his love for Israel. Though God had chosen Israel as a nation with whom he would have a particular relationship and over whom he would extend his kingship, he wanted the Israelites to know that his kingdom was much larger than the bounds of the land of promise and this small nation. He reminded them that the "whole earth" was his (Ex. 19:5). But while God emphasized to Israel the vastness of his rule, he simultaneously revealed to them the selectiveness of his particular affection for them. Although God is King over every nation, he particularly chose Israel as his precious people: "Although the whole earth is mine, you will be for me a kingdom of priests and a holy nation" (Ex. 19:6). Israel alone had the privilege of having a special covenant relationship with God.

Moses took this message to the people of Israel as he descended from the mountain. He conveyed "all the words" that God had commanded him to speak (Ex. 19:7) and the nation collectively responded, "We will do everything the LORD has said" (Ex. 19:8).

THE SECOND ASCENT

After the people had consented to obey the Lord, Moses returned to the mountaintop to share their answer with the Lord (Ex. 19:8). Then God did an extraordinary thing. God told Moses that he would take direct and explicit action to confirm Moses' exclusive ministry and his role as God's chosen mediator. "The LORD said to Moses, 'I am going to come to you in a dense cloud, so that the people will hear me speaking with you and will always put their trust in you' " (Ex. 19:9). God planned on endorsing Moses before all the people. What encouragement this must have brought to the heart of Moses! After all those challenges in the wilderness, the people of Israel should have had no doubt that Moses was their earthly leader and God's chosen prophet.

But there was more to God's message to Moses on this second ascent. God also gave Moses instructions regarding the need of the people to consecrate themselves. God commanded the people to take two days in preparation to meet with him (Ex. 19:10). They were to wash their clothes (Ex. 19:10). They were to be kept at a specified distance from the mountain and were warned not to touch it (Ex. 19:12). Anyone touching the foot of God's holy mountain would be stoned or shot with arrows (Ex. 19:13). Only Moses could touch that mountain.

Moses conveyed this message to the people and they obeyed God's instructions. Then on the morning of the third day, God did exactly what he promised:

> On the morning of the third day there was thunder and lightning, with a thick cloud over the mountain, and a very loud trumpet blast. Everyone in the camp

trembled. Then Moses led the people out of the camp to meet with God, and they stood at the foot of the mountain. Mount Sinai was covered with smoke, because the LORD descended on it in fire. The smoke billowed up from it like smoke from a furnace, and the whole mountain trembled violently. As the sound of the trumpet grew louder and louder, Moses spoke and the voice of God answered him. (Ex. 19:16–19)

God met with his people and spoke with his servant Moses in the presence of the entire trembling nation.

The second ascent of Moses thus prepared the way for the giving of the law by emphasizing two unequivocal points to Israel. First, God is holy and those who approach him must be holy. God emphasized this by requiring the people to consecrate themselves before meeting with him, and by prohibiting them from touching his holy mountain. Second, God also made it abundantly clear that he only spoke with and through Moses. After the theatrics of the thunder, lightning, and smoke, Moses spoke and the voice of God "answered him" (Ex. 19:9). God confirmed Moses as his mouthpiece to prepare the way for the giving of the law through him.

THE THIRD ASCENT

The final ascent recorded in Exodus 19 further emphasizes the holiness of God. In Exodus 19:20 God called Moses to the top of the mountain and told him to warn the people again that they must not attempt to push their way to the mountain in an effort to see the Lord. God declared that if the people attempted this they would perish (Ex. 19:21). He even warned the priests that if they were to serve in his presence they must consecrate themselves or perish (Ex. 19:22). Moses shared this message with the people.

After this last warning message, God spoke the words of his law to his people. He had set the stage by placing his law in the context of his deliverance of his people, his expectation of obedience, his setting them apart as his own special possession, and his teaching them about his uncompromising holiness. He had also set apart Moses as his sole spokesman and mediator. The people had fully consented to submit to the kingship of God.

THE TEN WORDS

As we come to briefly examine the substance of the Ten Commandments, it is vital that we keep in mind the context in which these imperatives were given to Israel. They were given to a delivered and redeemed people. This means that the Ten Commandments were not given as a means of earning redemption, but rather as a means of expressing gratitude for that redemption. God makes this clear in the prologue to the Commandments: "And God spoke all these words: 'I am the LORD your God, who brought you out of Egypt, out of the land of slavery'" (Ex. 20:1–2). God reminds Israel that he established his relationship with them by liberating them from the bondage they experienced in Egypt. As Mark Strom notes, "The Lord did not give the law to establish his relationship with the Israelites. He gave it because he already had a relationship with his people and he wanted them now to learn how to express this relationship faithfully."[1] The law was given to Israel because God loved his children and he wanted to instruct them regarding how to please him and how to live wisely and well in the land he was giving them.

First Commandment: A Call to Exclusivity
You shall have no other gods before me. (Ex. 20:3)

The First Commandment called Israel to covenantal fidelity with God. Much like in the human marriage relationship, God expected his people to forsake all other "gods" and to serve and love him exclusively. This expectation continues for believers in the new covenant. The moral law of God was not abolished through the coming of Jesus, but rather it was fulfilled; it was given its full meaning through his person and work (Matt. 5:17–18). Like Israel, we too are called into a covenantal relationship of exclusivity through the work of Jesus Christ. While most of us are not tempted to worship the pagan gods of old, we are constantly challenged by the false gods of our age—sex, money, power, luxury, pride, and self-worship.

How can we know if we are violating the First Commandment? Philip Ryken gives us a very helpful two-part test for this purpose.[2] First, Ryken notes that we need to ask ourselves, "What do we love?" We need to inquire of ourselves as to our passions and obsessions and ask if they are replacing God in our hearts. Second, Ryken calls us to ask ourselves, "What do you trust?" Where do you run when there is trouble? What gives you security?

The call for exclusive devotion to God has not changed with the coming of Christ. Jesus makes this abundantly clear in John 14:6 when he declares, "I am the way and the truth and the life. No one comes to the Father except through me."

Second Commandment: Regulated Worship

> You shall not make for yourself an image in the form
> of anything in heaven above or on the earth beneath
> or in the waters below. (Ex. 20:4)

The First Commandment instructed the people of Israel regarding *whom* they should worship; the Second Commandment informed them about *how* they should worship. The commandment prohibited them from making idols of any false god and of the one true God as well. This commandment serves as part of the scriptural foundation for what the Reformed tradition has termed the "regulative principle of worship." This principle states simply that

God has prescribed how we should worship him in the pages of Holy Scripture and we are not free to devise our own manner of worshipping him that is not authorized by Scripture.

Israel would struggle with this commandment throughout their long history. As we will see in the next chapter, they broke this commandment while they were still encamped at Sinai by making the golden calf (Ex. 32). But this proclivity toward idol making is not something restricted to Old Testament Israel. We still struggle with it today. While worship has changed drastically between the two testaments (i.e., the sacrificial system, temple, and priesthood have all been abrogated by God's express command), worship is still a matter that God regulates. It only makes sense that a sovereign God would regulate how we are to approach him. Of course, the core regulation of New Testament worship is that we can only approach God through our Great High Priest Jesus Christ. He is the only "image" of God that we are allowed to worship (Col. 1:15; Heb. 1:3). Jesus, in his exchange with the woman at the well in John 4, reiterated the heart of the Second Commandment when he declared how God is to be worshipped: "God is spirit, and his worshipers must worship in the Spirit and in truth" (John 4:24). NT

Third Commandment: Revering His Name

You shall not misuse the name of the Lord your God. (Ex. 20:7)

In chapter four, we witnessed God's revelation of his name ("I am") to Moses. One of the emphases of that chapter was the nexus between God's name and his character. Therefore, it should not surprise us that God demanded that Israel respect, regard, and revere his holy name. What does it mean to misuse God's name? Obviously, any profane use of God's name is a violation of this commandment. But the aim of the commandment is not just in forbidding profanity; it is also aimed at forbidding vanity. God also forbade the vain use of his name by attaching it to a false prophecy (Deut. 18:22), a false oath (Lev. 19:12), or using it as a magical incantation (Deut. 18:10–12). God's name should not be trifled with, invoked carelessly, or profaned in any manner.

This reverence for the name of God continues in the New Testament, but it takes on additional significance in the coming of Jesus Christ. The New Testament emphasizes the preciousness and power of the name of Jesus Christ. God has given Jesus the name above all names and it is at his name that every knee shall bow and every tongue shall confess that he is Lord (Phil. 2:9–11). The New Testament also stresses the importance of praying in Jesus' name (John 14:13), and believing in his name (Acts 16:31).

Like ancient Israel, we continue to be challenged by this commandment. While most Christians are successful in refraining from using Christ's name as a curse word, we often are less successful in avoiding the vain use of Christ's name. Sometimes we simply fail to invest the appropriate honor in the name of Christ by treating his name casually or flippantly. We fail to honor his name when we speak false promises, whether or not we actually take an oath (Matt. 5:33–37). We can even run the risk of treating his name like a magical incantation when we become flippant and superficial in our prayer lives. We are called to revere the name of the Lord Jesus Christ.

Fourth Commandment: The Lord of Time

Remember the Sabbath day by keeping it holy. (Ex. 20:6)

In this commandment God declared to Israel that he is the Lord of time. God pronounced dominion not just over one day, the seventh, but the other six as well. He told Israel to work for six days and then to set aside the seventh day for rest and worship. This pattern of six days of labor and one day of rest was set forth by God in his work of creation and he makes that connection explicit when he pronounces this commandment (Ex. 20:11). God declared his sovereignty over the entire life of Israel.

The continuing application of the Fourth Commandment is a much debated issue in the modern church. That is very unfortunate because it seems unlikely that any Christian would want to deny the underlying premise of this commandment—that God is Lord of all of life and that he has dominion over time. While we may disagree about the details of Sabbath observance in the modern church, we certainly cannot argue with the core calling of this commandment. We are called to worship and to rest, and we are reminded that our work, the other "six days," matter in the eyes of God. The commandment, of course, most importantly reminds us of the Sabbath rest that we find in the finished work of Jesus Christ (Matt. 11:28–30; Heb. 4:9–10). As with so much of the Old Testament law, the Fourth Commandment finds its meaning and fulfillment in the person and work of Jesus Christ.

Fifth Commandment: Honoring Authority

Honor your father and your mother. (Ex. 20:12)

With the Fifth Commandment we witness a turn to the topic of human relationships, but there is still a strong connection here to our relationship to God. In the Fifth Commandment, God addresses the human relationship that is most central to the continuation of the covenant through generations—the parent-child relationship. This relationship, of course, also serves as a reflection of God's relationship with us. God reveals himself as a father and gives us the privilege of addressing him in that manner (Gal. 4:6).[3]

The call to honor our parents is ultimately a call for us to respect those who are in authority over us. God is the ultimate authority to whom we are called to submit, but we are also in many human relationships where God has placed authorities over us, including the parent-child relationship. When we honor our parents we are ultimately honoring God. The New Testament continues to call us to honor our parents. Paul makes this explicit in Ephesians 6:1–3 when he says, "Children, obey your parents in the Lord, for this is right. 'Honor your father and mother'—which is the first commandment with a promise—'so that it may go well with you and that you may enjoy long life on the earth.' "

The Remainder of the Law Summarized

As previously noted, the Ten Commandments are divided between commandments related to our relationship with God and our relationships with others.[4] As we have seen, the first five commandments clearly set the boundaries and parameters of our interaction with God. The next four commandments (commandments six through nine) instruct Israel regarding how they should treat one another. Murder (Sixth Commandment), adultery (Seventh Commandment), theft (Eighth Commandment), and false testimony (Ninth Commandment) were all prohibited by God. With these commandments God reminded his people that loving their neighbors is as important as loving him because each human being is made in the image of God.

The final commandment prohibited the people of Israel from coveting goods, spouses, servants, animals, or any other items which belonged to their neighbors. Of all of the commandments, this is the one that penetrates most deeply into the thought and heart life of the Israelite. Though Jesus would ultimately apply all ten commandments to the area of the heart in his Sermon on the Mount (Matthew 5–7), the Ten Commandments, in their original redemptive-historical context, mainly focused on outward actions rather than on inward intentions.

The Tenth Commandment is the one exception because it targets the covetousness and greed which often spring forth from our hearts and minds. This final commandment foreshadows powerfully that God's ultimate concern in giving the law is to see our hearts changed toward him and toward our neighbor.

Like the first five commandments, the remaining five continue to apply to the lives of believers living in the new covenant era. The New Testament provides us with corollaries to each of the commandments as can be seen in the chart below:

Commandment	New Testament Corollary
You shall not murder. (Ex. 20:13)	You have heard that it was said to the people long ago, "You shall not murder, and anyone who murders will be subject to judgment." But I tell you that anyone who is angry with a brother or sister will be subject to judgment. Again, anyone who says to a brother or sister, "Raca," is answerable to the court. And anyone who says, "You fool!" will be in danger of the fire of hell. (Matt. 5:21–22)
You shall not commit adultery. (Ex. 20:14)	You have heard that it was said, "You shall not commit adultery." But I tell you that anyone who looks at a woman lustfully has already committed adultery with her in his heart. (Matt. 5:27–28)
You shall not steal. (Ex. 20:15)	Anyone who has been stealing must steal no longer, but must work, doing something useful with their own hands, that they may have something to share with those in need. (Eph. 4:28)

[handwritten margin note: How we relate to comm.]

Commandment	New Testament Corollary
You shall not give false testimony against your neighbor. (Ex. 20:16)	You were taught, with regard to your former way of life, to put off your old self, which is being corrupted by its deceitful desires; to be made new in the attitude of your minds; and to put on the new self, created to be like God in true righteousness and holiness. Therefore each of you must put off falsehood and speak truthfully to your neighbor, for we are all members of one body. (Eph. 4:22–25)
You shall not covet your neighbor's house. You shall not covet your neighbor's wife, or his male or female servant, his ox or donkey, or anything that belongs to your neighbor. (Ex. 20:12–17)	For it is from within, _out of a person's heart_, that evil thoughts come—sexual immorality, theft, murder, adultery, greed (ESV = "coveting"), malice, deceit, lewdness, envy, slander, arrogance and folly. (Mark 7:21–22)

The giving of the law at Sinai is one of the most significant redemptive-historical events in all of Scripture. God, through his servant Moses, set forth the foundation of his redemptive relationship with the nation of Israel and his expectations of how they would approach him and treat one another. There was no negotiation of terms. God as the Sovereign King established the parameters of his relationship with his people. Though the Ten Commandments must be understood in their unique original redemptive and covenantal context, we have seen that their substance is ultimately a reflection of God's eternal moral law which continues to apply to believers today. Like so much of the Old Testament revelation, the Ten Commandments can only be fully understood through the person and work of

Jesus Christ. Accordingly, it should not surprise us that Jesus gave the best summary of the heart of these commandments when he responded to the question, "Teacher, which is the greatest commandment in the Law?" (Matt. 22:36), by replying:

> "Love the Lord your God with all your heart and with all your soul and with all your mind." This is the first and greatest commandment. And the second is like it: "Love your neighbor as yourself." All the Law and the Prophets hang on these two commandments. (Matt. 22:37–40)

But the greatest gift that Jesus gave to his people was not his exegesis and distillation of the law; rather, it was his own perfect life lived in fulfillment of that law on our behalf. This is something Moses could not have done on behalf of his people. It is important for us to remember that our redemption was secured not only through Jesus' death on the cross, but also through the righteous life that he lived upon this earth. Jesus lived for our salvation as much as he died for it. Without the life and death of Jesus, the law that came through Moses could only bring condemnation and death to us. But by Jesus' perfect obedience imputed to us and by his perfect sacrificial death on our behalf, Jesus accomplished what the law never could—he made his people righteous and holy:

> For what the law was powerless to do because it was weakened by the flesh, God did by sending his own Son in the likeness of sinful flesh to be a sin offering. And so he condemned sin in the flesh, in order that the righteous requirement of the law might be fully met in us, who do not live according to the flesh but according to the Spirit. (Rom. 8:3–4)

Moses was the human vessel that God chose to communicate his law to his people, but Jesus was the one who

129

fulfilled that law, both in meaning and in practice. The law that was given through Moses could only bring death, but the law fulfilled by Jesus brings life and liberty. This is perhaps the greatest contrast between these two mediators. As the apostle John reminds us, "For the law was given through Moses; grace and truth came through Jesus Christ" (John 1:17).

THE TABERNACLE

Though the Ten Commandments usually garner most of our theological reflection and attention when it comes to the giving of God's law, we should not forget that the commands and instructions God provided to his people at Sinai extended beyond the Ten Commandments. It is easy to forget that in the remainder of the book of Exodus, from chapter 19 forward, Israel remains encamped around Sinai. There was much more that God wanted to teach them than what is contained in the Ten Commandments, some of which is itemized in Exodus 20–23. The most significant additional area that God addressed was how his people should worship him. The bulk of this instruction was focused upon the construction of the tabernacle. As with the Ten Commandments, God mediated these lessons through his servant Moses.

The tabernacle demonstrates a powerful and wonderful aspect of God's covenantal relationship with his people. God promised to be with his people—and not merely in an abstract way. God promised his very presence to his people. At the core of God's covenant promise is not only that he will be our God and we his people, but also that he will "walk among" us (Lev. 26:12). God promised Israel that he would dwell among them.

But there was a basic problem that God faced in fulfilling that promise and that problem was us. There was a time when God could dwell with humans because we were created without sin. Thus, we see God walking amid the garden with Adam and Eve. But after the fall, this all changed. Israel was certainly not without sin. But God found a way to dwell with his people by building a tabernacle, a tent where he could meet with Israel. God shared his plans for the tabernacle with Moses (Ex. 25–30) and he gave very detailed instructions regarding its construction (Ex. 35–40).

Regulated by God

As we saw with the Second Commandment, in providing plans for the tabernacle God was once again demonstrating that he regulates how he is to be worshipped. God gave Moses very specific instructions regarding how the people were to approach him in worship. In other words, God regulated his own worship. As Graeme Goldsworthy notes, "No detail in the construction of the tent and its contents is left to the imagination of the people, for they are completely dependent upon the revelation of God for knowledge of their relationship to him."[5]

Involving His People

Although God devised the plans for the construction of the tabernacle, he did call his people to share in and contribute to its actual construction. First, the people were called upon to contribute materials necessary for the construction of the tabernacle (Ex. 25:1–7). When Moses brought this requirement to the people (Ex. 35:4–9), they responded in great faithfulness and generosity (Ex. 35:20–27). In fact, the people responded with such generosity that they actually gave more than was necessary (Ex. 36:3–7).

A second way in which God enlisted his people in the construction of the tabernacle was his call for the employment of specific skilled craftsmen (Ex. 31:1–11). Two men were set apart by God for particular recognition, Bezalel and Oholiab (Ex. 31:3). These two men displayed particular

THE LAW CAME THROUGH MOSES

skill and their gifts were used by God in completing the tabernacle (Ex. 35:34).

Central to Israel's Life

By God's design, the tabernacle was placed in the center of the camp with the twelve tribes situated around it. The centrality of the tabernacle to the life of Israel was purposeful. The tabernacle was a constant reminder to Israel that God was to be at the center of their lives.

The physical construction of the tabernacle also reminded Israel of the holiness of God and their need of mediation to approach to him. The tabernacle served to distinguish between the holy and the common. For example, the tabernacle was surrounded by a fence which served to create an inner courtyard. This reminded the Israelites that they did not have unfettered access to God because of their sinfulness. Another reminder of their sinfulness was the fact that an altar was present inside the courtyard and that a priest would have to mediate for the people. The people could only have access to God through sacrifice and through his appointed priesthood.

The inside of the tabernacle only served to further emphasize God's holiness. The basic structure of the interior of the tabernacle included a division, separated by a veil, between the Holy Place and the Most Holy Place. The Most Holy Place was where the ark of the covenant resided. The ark was, in essence, God's throne, or perhaps better stated, his footstool (see Ps. 99:1–5). Only the high priest could enter the Most Holy Place and then only once a year. The high priest also was required to make careful preparation before entering the Most Holy Place.

The tabernacle was a constant physical lesson to Israel. As Graeme Goldsworthy writes, "Everything about this structure speaks of three great truths: God wills to dwell among his people and to meet with them; sin separates people from God; and God provides a way of reconciliation through sacrifice and the mediatorial office of the priest."[6] The tabernacle spoke volumes to God's people.

The True Tabernacle

Of course, the greatest function that the tabernacle served was in foreshadowing the ultimate dwelling of God with men through the incarnation of Jesus Christ. As John declares in his Gospel, "The Word became flesh and made his dwelling among us. We have seen his glory, the glory of the one and only Son, who came from the Father, full of grace and truth" (John 1:14). The word translated "dwelling" in this verse is related to the concept of tent or tabernacle. Jesus became the tabernacle par excellence. Later in Israel's history, after they settled in the land of promise, the tabernacle was replaced with a fixed temple. Jesus also fulfills this imagery and directly connects his own body to the temple (John 2:19).

But the connections between Jesus and the Old Testament tabernacle do not end with his incarnation. The New Testament also teaches us that the veil that denied access to the Most Holy Place was torn during the crucifixion of Jesus (Matt. 27:51). In other words, Jesus, through his sacrificial death, removed the barrier between God and sinner (Heb. 9). Jesus also replaces the sacrifice that was required in the tabernacle and the priesthood that mediated on behalf of the people (Heb. 4:14).

If all of this were not marvelous enough, Jesus fulfills the covenant promise of dwelling with us even after his resurrection and ascension. Prior to ascending, Jesus promised his church the indwelling of the Holy Spirit. Through his redemptive work on our behalf, the people of God actually have the privilege of being God's dwelling place. Jesus made it possible for his people to be the tabernacle or temple of God. Thus, Paul urges the saints at Corinth toward holiness by these words:

> Do you not know that your bodies are temples of the Holy Spirit who is in you, whom you have received from God? You are not your own; you were bought at a price. Therefore honor God with your bodies. (1 Cor. 6:19–20)

133

Jesus is Emmanuel. He is God with us. God first demonstrated this reality to his people through the construction
of the tabernacle and he fully revealed it to them through
the tent of the flesh of his Son.

THE LAW AND TABERNACLE
COALESCE IN CHRIST

After surveying the magnitude and significance of the
giving of God's law and the construction of the tabernacle,
we can understand why Moses is regarded as the greatest
among the Old Testament figures. God gave his law through
Moses and he gave the plans for the tabernacle through
Moses. Moses mediated these realities to the people of
God. What an extraordinary privilege!

But Moses' privilege was not ultimately found in his
role of mediator. His great privilege was that he was truly
a preacher of Jesus Christ. While he was not fully aware
of this service, he was ultimately pointing to Christ when
he shared the law with Israel and when he worked on the
tabernacle. For, as we have seen, the law and the tabernacle coalesce in the person and work of Jesus Christ.
Jesus exegetes, clarifies, and expands on the meaning
of the law. Even more importantly, he actually fulfills it
through his active obedience. In addition, Jesus becomes
the fulfillment of God's promise to dwell among his people
by "tabernacling" among us. It is Jesus who now resides in
the center of our lives and serves as a constant reminder
to his people of God's holiness, their need of a mediator,
and their glorious redemption from bondage to sin.

FOR FURTHER REFLECTION

1. When Israel arrived at Mount Sinai, Moses made
   three ascents to the top of the mountain. What

do we learn about God and his relationship to his people from each of these ascents?

2. What does the prologue to the Ten Commandments reveal about the role of the law in God's relationship with his people?

3. What is the core teaching of each of the first five commandments? *r/t God*

4. What distinction can be drawn between the first five commandments and commandments six through ten? *r/t others*

5. Do the Ten Commandments continue to apply to the lives of New Testament believers? Can you find New Testament support for each commandment? Are there are differences with regard to how we relate to the Ten Commandments and how Old Testament Israel related to them? *noted*

6. What three spiritual lessons are taught by the structure and location of the tabernacle?

7. Who is the true tabernacle of God? How does this reality relate to us? *Jesus indwells us-HS*

8. How do the law and tabernacle coalesce in the person and work of Jesus Christ? *He fulfills the law*

God wants to dwell w/ them   obedience

Sin seperates from Him

They need sacrifices + a priest to bridge the seperation of man → God.

CHAPTER TEN

FROM IDOLATRY TO GLORY

Exodus 32–34

Sometimes life can feel like an emotional roller coaster. We can be in the midst of experiencing the heights of joy over some wonderful news only to soon find ourselves plummeting to the valley of discouragement. Of course, it often works in the exact opposite direction as well; we are stuck in a valley of discouragement and then something happens which lifts us to new heights. Moses' life, like our own lives, included both types of experiences.

As we have seen, Moses began his young adulthood on a great high as a son in Pharaoh's house, but he soon plummeted to a new low when he fled from Egypt as a fugitive after killing the Egyptian man. But now we find Moses experiencing the exact opposite. In this chapter, we will see Moses at a new low of discouragement regarding the people of Israel, but then he is lifted up to extraordinary heights by God's self-revelation. We will see Moses' journey from the low of Israel's idolatry to the height of God's glory.

THE GOLDEN CALF

As we saw in the previous chapter, God brought the nation of Israel to Mount Sinai to enter into covenant with them. That covenant relationship was predicated on God's deliverance of Israel from Egypt. As Israel's King, God set forth stipulations of his relationship with Israel which find their most succinct expression in the Ten Commandments (Ex. 20). As we come to Exodus 32, Moses is once again ascending the mountain to meet with God. The purpose of Moses' visit was to bring down the tablets of the law. Israel was on the cusp of receiving a written affirmation of their covenant with God. This was meant to be a high point in their history. Unfortunately, it soon turned into what is arguably Israel's lowest spiritual moment.

What led to this spiritual low? The people simply grew impatient. In their opinion, Moses was taking too long. Where was he? They grew restless. Then they found Aaron and surrounded him and declared, "Come, make us gods who will go before us. As for this fellow Moses who brought us up out of Egypt, we don't know what has happened to him" (Ex. 32:1). One would have expected that Aaron would have chastised the Israelites for making such a request. After all, such an act would be a violation of at least the first two of the Ten Commandments. But Aaron provided no resistance. He caved in to the pressure of the masses gathered around him and stated, "Take off the gold earrings that your wives, your sons and your daughters are wearing, and bring them to me" (Ex. 32:2).

After gathering the gold from the people, Aaron fashioned it into the shape of a calf. When the people saw it they proclaimed, "These are your gods, Israel, who brought you up out of Egypt" (Ex. 32:4). Aaron proclaimed that a feast would be held on the following day and the next day the people "sat down to eat and drink and got up to indulge in revelry" (Ex. 32:5-6). Israel was having a feast to the idol they had made.

While Israel's deeds were unknown to Moses, they were fully known to God. God revealed to Moses what the people were doing:

Then the LORD said to Moses, "Go down, because your people, whom you brought up out of Egypt, have become corrupt. They have been quick to turn away from what I commanded them and have made themselves an idol cast in the shape of a calf. They have bowed down to it and sacrificed to it and have said, 'These are your gods, Israel, who brought you up out of Egypt.'" (Ex. 32:7–8)

He then pronounced his desire to punish Israel:

"I have seen these people," the LORD said to Moses, "and they are a stiff-necked people. Now leave me alone so that my anger may burn against them and that I may destroy them. Then I will make you into a great nation." (Ex. 32:9–10)

God was ready to dispense with Israel and start over again.

A MAN OF MERCY

One might think that Moses would have taken this opportunity to concur with God's judgment against Israel. After all, these people had continually rebelled and grumbled against him! Didn't they fully deserve God's wrath? They were breaking the very covenant that Moses was planning on bringing to them on the tablets of stone. But Moses did not call for Israel's demise; rather, he interceded on her behalf:

But Moses sought the favor of the LORD his God. "LORD," he said, "why should your anger burn against your people, whom you brought out of Egypt with great power and a mighty hand? Why should the Egyptians say, 'It was with evil intent that he brought them out, to kill them in the mountains and to wipe them off the face of the earth'? Turn from your fierce anger; relent and do not bring disaster on your people. Remember your servants Abraham, Isaac and Israel, to whom you swore by your own self: 'I will make your descendants as numerous as the stars in the sky and I will give your descendants all this land I promised them, and it will be their inheritance forever.' " (Ex. 32:11–13)

Moses pleaded for mercy for his people and the manner in which he made this plea not only reflects his spiritual maturity, but also serves as a continuing pattern for prayer.

God had offered Moses a most attractive alternative of starting over with a new nation with Moses as its appointed leader. This offer was both a condemnation of Israel and an affirmation of Moses. But when Moses launches into his intercession on Israel's behalf, he does not focus on either himself or Israel, instead he focuses on God's glory. He explains to God that the destruction of Israel would allow Egypt to question his deeds and to sully his reputation. Moses' concern was not for himself or his own glory; his concern was not even for the safety of the people he had been leading. His concern was for preserving and protecting the name of God. He was fulfilling the Third Commandment. Our prayers should always begin with a focus on the glory of God's name and character and not our own glory and needs.

Moses also based his plea not on any good thing he had done, but rather, solely upon God's revealed will and promises. Moses asked God to remember the covenant promises that he had made to Abraham, Isaac, and Israel. He set his plea upon the bedrock of God's covenant and his self-attesting oath to bring Israel to the land of promise. Our prayers should always be offered based on our covenant relationship with God and our requests couched within the context of God's promises to us.

While the golden calf incident was certainly a low point for Israel, it was for Moses one of his most exemplary moments. Here Moses displayed the heart of a mediator as he interceded on behalf of sinful Israel. He offered a selfless prayer focused on preserving God's glory. He endeavored to turn God's wrath to peace, and God accepted Moses' efforts: "Then the LORD relented and did not bring on his people the disaster he had threatened" (Ex. 32:14).[1] Of course, we must remember that God is the ultimate source of mercy in this account. God could have exercised his judgment upon Israel without involving Moses, but God purposefully involved Moses to allow him the opportunity to intercede on behalf of his people. While God was the ultimate source of Israel's salvation, Moses' actions should not be diminished. Moses was faithful to his calling as mediator and was instrumental in saving his nation from utter ruin. Moses showed himself to be a man of mercy.

A MAN IN CHARGE

Moses' efforts to secure mercy for Israel did not mean he was not upset with the scandalous behavior of the Israelites. The Bible declares that when Moses actually saw the golden calf and the people dancing around it, "his anger burned" (Ex. 32:19). More than that, Moses was so upset that he threw the tablets out of his hands; they crashed to the ground and broke into pieces. This action was more than a mere expression of frustration on Moses' part; it was an act of legal significance, similar to the tearing up of a modern contract. Israel had broken God's covenant.

But Moses was not finished displaying his indignation over Israel's idolatry. After throwing the tablets to the ground, he then took the golden calf and ground it to a powder. He mixed the ground up remains of the calf with water and made the Israelites drink it (Ex. 32:20). He then confronted Aaron and angrily inquired, "What did these people do to you, that you led them into such great sin?" (Ex. 32:21). After confronting Aaron, Moses next dealt with the people by ascertaining those whose allegiance was with God. He stood at the entrance of the camp and he stated, "Whoever is for the LORD, come to me" (Ex. 32:26). The Levites quickly rallied to Moses.

But not everyone chose to serve the Lord that day. Moses was then faced with a difficult task. There were certain people in the camp who would not repent of their sin of idolatry. Moses needed to act decisively to rid the camp of this sin. He enlisted the Levites to preserve the holiness of God's people and commanded them to kill all those who had not rallied to the side of the Lord. Scripture states that about three thousand people died that day, and some of them were the family members and neighbors of the Levites who were executing the sentence (Ex. 32:28).

This is admittedly a difficult text for us to understand in a twenty-first-century context. It strikes us as a harsh punishment for three thousand people to die for idolatry. Why was this slaughter necessary? We must remember that the issue at hand here was a blatant violation of the first three commandments. The problem here was sin. Those who were slain failed to love exclusively the one true God, had created an idol, and were failing to revere God's name. Sometimes we simply take sin too lightly. The Scriptures are clear that the wages of sin—of any and all sin, no matter how small or large—is death (Rom. 6:23). Israel was called to be a pure and holy people exclusively set apart to God; the presence of idolaters among them made this impossible. Through their blatant sin, they had earned its wages.

As new covenant believers, we likely see this incident as harsh, but we should be careful to remember that though such forms of punishment for idolatry are not prescribed in the new covenant era, the underlying antithesis between believer and nonbeliever continues with us today. Much like Old Testament Israel, the new covenant church cannot tolerate idolatry, and its officers and leaders must eliminate it. We don't use swords like the Levites, but we do use the power of church discipline to preserve the holiness of God's people. We must remember that Jesus issued a similar rallying call of allegiance in Matthew 12:30: "Whoever is not with me is against me." There is no middle ground when it comes to our allegiance to God. We are either with him or against him.

While the slaying of the idolaters remains difficult for us to fully understand, it does demonstrate the leadership skills of Moses. He had pleaded for mercy for those who had committed the sin of idolatry but were repentant. However, when it came to the unrepentant, Moses took action that preserved God's name and Israel's holy calling. Here we see Moses taking charge and making the hard decisions required of a leader of a holy people.

Moses did what he had to do. He displayed an appropriate righteous anger over what the Israelites had done. By doing so Moses foreshadowed the righteous anger of Jesus as he turned over the tables of the moneychangers in the temple (Matt. 21:12). He confronted Aaron on his failure of leadership. He confronted Israel regarding its sin. He called the people to serve the Lord, and he dealt with those who would not ally themselves with God. He demonstrated that he could mete out judgment as well as mercy. Through his decisive actions Moses showed that he was a man in charge.

A MAN LIKE CHRIST

The day after the three thousand had died, Moses addressed the people again. He continued his skilled leadership by confronting Israel once again for their sin, but also informing them that he would attempt to intercede on their behalf. "The next day Moses said to the people, 'You have committed a great sin. But now I will go up to the LORD; perhaps I can make atonement for your sin' " (Ex. 32:30).

Moses once again ascended the mountain and spoke with the Lord. Previously, Moses had stayed God's hand of judgment by pleading for mercy. He had based that plea on God's covenant promises made to the patriarchs. This time Moses took his efforts of intercession a step further and even personalized them:

> So Moses went back to the LORD and said, "Oh, what a great sin these people have committed! They have made themselves gods of gold. But now, please forgive their sin—but if not, then blot me out of the book you have written." (Ex. 32:32)

Moses offers his own life to secure God's forgiveness and in this moment he foreshadows brilliantly the person and work of Jesus Christ.

Moses had been rejected by Israel, yet he was willing to give himself for her. God, of course, did not require this of Moses. He forgave Israel's sin and Moses remained Israel's leader. But Moses' offer points us to Jesus. Like Moses, Jesus was widely rejected by his own people. They had once worshipped him as the coming Messiah, placing palm branches of victory in his path in his triumphal entry into Jerusalem. But they quickly turned against him and demanded his crucifixion at the hands of Pontius Pilate. Upon the cross, Jesus showed compassion on the very people who had demanded his crucifixion. "Father, forgive them, for they do not know what they do" (Luke 23:34).

Both Moses and Jesus were willing to give their lives for the sins of God's people, but the major difference was that the offering that Jesus made was efficacious in all respects. Moses' offer, while displaying the heart of a mediator, could not atone for the sin of God's chosen people. In stark contrast, Jesus' offering of himself was fully efficacious to atone for the sin of God's chosen people. Moses' heart was in the right place; he simply lacked the requisite righteousness to satisfy God's holy standard.

In the account of Israel's sin of idolatry with the golden calf, we witness Moses at his best. Here Moses serves as a merciful mediator and just leader. He mixes together judgment and mercy in just the right proportions. He is even willing to give himself to secure the protection of his people. Of course, what we really witness here is Moses fulfilling his greatest role of typifying and foreshadowing Jesus and his work. Moses was a man like Christ.

DESIRING TO SEE HIS GLORY

After the disaster of the golden calf, Moses must have been both physically exhausted and spiritually discouraged. He had just witnessed the fickleness of God's people and the consequences of idolatry. Israel's idolatry had a profound impact on Moses and also on God's relationship with his people. The beginning of Exodus 33 reveals that because of Israel's idolatry God decided to withdraw his presence from his people. God ordered Moses to establish a "tent of meeting" outside the camp of Israel so that God could meet with Moses and be separated from the Israelites (Ex. 33:7).

This tent of meeting was a place that demarcated God's separation from his people, who had made their camp unclean by their idolatry. For the people of Israel, the tent of meeting resulted in a loss of intimacy with God, but for Moses the experience was quite the opposite. Moses continued to meet with God with increasing intimacy during this time. Scripture references this intimacy in Exodus 33:11: "The LORD would speak to Moses face to face, as one speaks to a friend." The golden calf incident caused a clear rift between God and his people, but Moses was God's loyal servant and friend. God was distancing himself from Israel, but growing closer to Moses.

145

THE DESIRE OF MOSES' HEART

It is during these visits with God at the tent of meeting that we get an incredibly revealing glimpse into Moses' heart. In some ways, Moses revisited his encounter with God in the wilderness where, at the burning bush, he inquired after God's name and God revealed himself to Moses as "I AM." At that point, Moses needed the reassurance that he could carry out the task of returning to his people and be their leader. He needed to know more about God and he begged for God's self-revelation. God granted it.

Now Moses was bearing the full weight of his leadership of Israel. He had witnessed the triumphs and tragedies of Israel's initial wanderings in the wilderness. They had traversed far, but were still not in the land of promise (and he did not yet know that it would take them another forty years to get there). Now Moses was alone again in the wilderness with God. He was longing for a deeper knowledge of God. He again yearned for God to reveal himself in a powerful way:

> Moses said to the LORD, "You have been telling me, 'Lead these people,' but you have not let me know whom you will send with me. You have said, 'I know you by name and you have found favor with me.' If you are pleased with me, teach me your ways so I may know you and continue to find favor with you. Remember that this nation is your people." (Ex. 33:12–13)

Moses wanted more of God. He wanted to understand what God was doing and to peer into his plans. He also wanted to make sure that God would be with him as he led the people to the land of promise.

God responded by promising that his presence would go with Moses and the people (Ex. 33:14). This must have

146

greatly reassured Moses, because he now understood that without God's presence his efforts would fail. God promised that he would do everything Moses asked because he was pleased with Moses and knew him by name.

It was at this moment of deep intimacy that Moses made his boldest request of God. He not only wanted God's presence to be with Israel, but he also wanted to experience God's presence on a personal level and in a unique way. Moses said to God, "Now show me your glory" (Ex. 33:18).

What exactly did Moses want to see? After all, he had seen the ten plagues, the parting of the Red Sea, and the destruction of the Egyptians. What more did he need? But Moses did not ask to see God's power here. He had seen that sure enough. He wanted to see God's glory. He wanted to experience the weightiness of God. He wanted to experience fully the splendor of God's presence on a personal level. He was begging God for a unique form of self-disclosure and self-revelation. He was asking God for something that God had not granted to any human since the garden of Eden. He wanted full and unfettered access to the resplendent glory of God! This was the desire of Moses' heart.

GOD'S GRACIOUS ACCOMMODATION

What Moses was asking for was a wonderful thing and it reflected where his heart was spiritually. He wanted more of God. He wanted to know God. These were commendable desires. There was only one problem—if God granted Moses' request it would have killed Moses. God explained to Moses:

> "I will cause all my goodness to pass in front of you, and I will proclaim my name, the LORD, in your presence. I will have mercy on whom I will have mercy, and I will have compassion on whom I will

have compassion. But," he said, "you cannot see my face, for no one may see me and live." (Ex. 33:19–20)

God could not allow Moses to have what he desired, but he promised him all the glory he could grant Moses to see without killing him:

Then the LORD said, "There is a place near me where you may stand on a rock. When my glory passes by, I will put you in a cleft in the rock and cover you with my hand until I have passed by. Then I will remove my hand and you will see my back; but my face must not be seen." (Ex. 33:21–23)

God promised Moses a glimpse of his glory and beauty.

SEEING THE GLORY OF GOD

The fulfillment of God's promise to Moses occurs in Exodus 34. This chapter is in many ways a recapitulation of Exodus 19–20 and the original giving of the law at Sinai. Moses once again ascends Mount Sinai to receive the two tablets of the law. During this meeting God reveals himself to Moses:

Then the LORD came down in the cloud and stood there with him and proclaimed his name, the LORD. And he passed in front of Moses, proclaiming, "The LORD, the LORD, the compassionate and gracious God, slow to anger, abounding in love and faithfulness, maintaining love to thousands, and forgiving wickedness, rebellion and sin. Yet he does not leave the guilty unpunished; he punishes the children and their children for the sin of the parents to the third and fourth generation." (Ex. 34:5–7)

God's revelation was twofold. First, he revealed his glory in a physical manner by passing in front of Moses. Moses could see God's veiled glory. But there was more than just seeing here. God also spoke to Moses. He revealed his glory through sight and sound. God's voice spoke to Moses and shared words which express the very heart of God's character, much like the "I AM" declaration of Exodus 3:13–15. The revelation of God's covenant character as being a compassionate, gracious, slow to anger, abounding in love, and forgiving God is just as profound as the "I AM" declaration. The words that God spoke as he passed in front of Moses reveal so much about God's character and nature that they are repeated numerous times throughout the Old Testament (e.g., Num. 14:18; Neh. 9:17; Pss. 103:8, 17; 145:8; Jer. 32:18–19; Joel 2:13; Jonah 4:2). Moses both saw and heard God's glory.

This revelation left Moses fundamentally changed. Something profound had occurred on that day. This was reflected in Moses' own appearance. When he descended from Mount Sinai with the two tablets of the covenant in his hands, his face was visibly radiant (Ex. 34:29). When the people saw this they were afraid to even approach Moses (Ex. 34:30). Moses had seen and heard the glory of God and he was transfigured by it.

UPON ANOTHER MOUNT

Like so many experiences in Moses' life, this episode also serves to point us to the one greater than Moses. Moses desired unfettered access to God and to see his full glory, but Moses could not see that because he was a sinner. His heart was in the right place, but he was simply incapable of dwelling in the unveiled presence of a holy God. He desired an intimacy that he could not have. Jesus, on the other hand, does experience this type of intimacy as part of the communion of the triune God. Jesus as the mediator of a new and better covenant sits at the very right hand of God. As the eternal Son of God and as the Son of Man, Jesus fully experiences the glory of God. Something Moses could never do during his days in Israel.

But the distinction between Jesus and Moses is even greater on this point. For Jesus not only experiences the full glory of God, he also inherently possesses this glory as a member of the Godhead. Moses' face may have been made radiant by the glory of God, but this was wholly a derivative experience. Moses was reflecting God's glory. The glory of Jesus is inherent. It is his glory. Jesus is the glory of God. As the writer to the Hebrews proclaims, "The Son is the radiance of God's glory and the exact representation of his being" (Heb. 1:3).

In the New Testament, at the Mount of Transfiguration, we witness a parallel experience to what occurred in Exodus 34. In this incident, Jesus, like Moses, ascended a mountain where the light of God's glory was visible and God's voice was heard. Jesus' face "shone like the sun, and his clothes became as white as the light" (Matt. 17:2). God's voice boomed in affirmation and love for his Son, "This is my Son, whom I love; with him I am well pleased. Listen to him!" (Matt. 17:5). But Jesus was not alone on that mountain. Two men were seen with him—Elijah and Moses.

While Moses must have been awed by his experience on Mount Sinai when he saw God's glory and his face was radiant, this was really nothing compared to the privilege that God gave Moses at the Mount of Transfiguration. For there on that latter mountain Moses saw the full glory of God in the face of Jesus Christ. The amazing thing for us is that we, as believers, all have the privilege of seeing God's glory as revealed through the person, work, and word of Jesus Christ. "The Word became flesh and made his dwelling among us. We have seen his glory, the glory of the One and Only, who came from the Father, full of grace and truth" (John 1:14).

FOR FURTHER REFLECTION

1. Why did Israel demand the golden calf?
2. What three things do we learn about Moses' character from how he responded to the incident of the golden calf?
3. What was the desire of Moses' heart? What did this reveal about his relationship with God?
4. How did God accommodate Moses' desire? What does this reveal about God and his relationship with Moses?
5. How does the Mount of Transfiguration relate to Moses' desire to see the glory of God?

Saw Jesus fully

EPILOGUE

The Story of Continues

As we have seen, the life of Moses, as revealed in the pages of the book of Exodus, was certainly extraordinary. Moses began his life under a death sentence. He was raised a prince in Pharaoh's house. He became a fugitive after his murder of the Egyptian. He spent forty years in the desert working as a shepherd. He became God's mediator. As God's servant, he pronounced the plagues upon Egypt, faced the army of Pharaoh head on, and oversaw God's parting of the Red Sea. Moses led his people through the wilderness, heard their grumbling, and watched God provide for them with water, manna, and quail. He ascended Mount Sinai and spoke with God. He ate with God. He received and declared the law of God. He saw the idolatry of Israel and the veiled glory of God. What a remarkable life!

But the story of Moses does not end with the closing of the book of Exodus. His story continues throughout the remainder of the Pentateuch, the first five books of the Bible. While an exhaustive examination of Moses' life revealed in these books is beyond the scope of this work, some brief highlighting of what occurred in the remainder of his life is warranted if we are to grasp the full nature of his story.

MUTINY IN THE DESERT (NUMBERS 12)

Moses was always dealing with some complaint against his leadership. We have already seen how the Israelites grumbled and complained against him, particularly during the wilderness wanderings. These personal attacks against him must have been painful for Moses. Anyone who has ever had a leadership position knows the pain of such criticisms and rejections.

But while criticism and rejection is difficult to take in general, it is particularly acute if the attack comes from someone close to you. Moses experienced this type of personal attack in his life. He was the target of a conspiracy against his leadership that was hatched by his sister Miriam and embraced by his brother Aaron.

The conspiracy was birthed in Miriam's resentment of Moses' wife, Zipporah. Zipporah was the daughter of the priest Jethro. She was not a Hebrew. She was also a very strong-willed and powerful woman. One only need read the account of how she took charge and circumcised Moses' sons when he had not done so (Ex. 4:24–26) to understand her character.

Zipporah had not been with Moses during the Exodus, but met up with him as he was approaching Sinai, and her arrival threatened Miriam. Before Zipporah came on the scene, Miriam had been the undisputed leader among the women of Israel. Zipporah threatened that claim.

We must remember that Miriam had some reasons to expect to be in a privileged status. In addition to being Moses' sister, she had been integral to the preservation of Moses' life as a child, served alongside Moses and Aaron during the wilderness wanderings, and led the women in song after the victory at the Red Sea. But she could not control her jealousy and this led her to hatch a conspiracy against Moses.

Miriam conspired with her brother Aaron to challenge Moses' faithfulness for having married a non-Hebrew woman, something which Hebrews were forbidden to do. Zipporah was a Cushite. Miriam clearly instigated this conspiracy, which is evidenced by the fact that her name appears first in the biblical description of the conspiracy:

"Miriam and Aaron began to talk against Moses because of his Cushite wife, for he had married a Cushite" (Num. 12:1). In Numbers 12:2, we see clearly the jealousy of Miriam and Aaron against Moses: " 'Has the LORD spoken only through Moses?' they asked. 'Hasn't he also spoken through us?' "

God quickly nipped this conspiracy in the bud by summoning Moses, Aaron, and Miriam to appear before him (Num. 12:4). There God defended the authority of Moses. God declared the special role that only Moses possessed: "With him I speak face to face, clearly and not in riddles; he sees the form of the LORD. Why then were you not afraid to speak against my servant Moses?" (Num. 12:8).

God punished Miriam by striking her with leprosy (Num. 12:10), but amazingly Moses interceded on her behalf. He cried out, "Please, God, heal her!" (Num. 12:13). God responded to Moses' intercession by changing Miriam's punishment from leprosy to being exiled from the camp for seven days (Num. 12:14).

This challenge against Moses from his own family members must have struck a blow to his heart. It must have been extraordinarily painful. But both the experience of this betrayal and his reaction to it reveal how Christlike he had become. First, like Jesus, Moses experienced betrayal within his inner circle. Jesus would later experience this type of betrayal, on a much larger scale, from Judas. Like Miriam, Judas was in the inner circle and shared the table with Jesus. Moses' experience with Miriam foreshadows the betrayal Christ would endure at the hand of Judas.

But Moses' response to this betrayal also reveals his Christlikeness. He loved his enemies. He graciously interceded on Miriam's behalf and saved her from the scourge of leprosy. This displays the maturity of Moses' heart. Like Jesus, he forgave those who were enemies. Even in the midst of a mutiny against him, Moses showed himself a worthy servant and a faithful mediator.

A LESSON FORGOTTEN (NUMBERS 20)

One of Moses' early failings was his pride. That was most clearly evident in his murdering of the Egyptian man who was attacking one of his Hebrew brothers. We saw how this act displayed that Moses was forcing God's timing regarding Moses' role as leader of Israel and appropriating the prerogatives of God to himself. It took Moses forty years in the desert to have that prideful attitude removed. After his time in the desert, Moses emerged as a much more humble servant.

But Moses' bouts with pride were not over. Later in life, as Israel neared entering the land of promise, he repeated some of his early mistakes and it cost him dearly. The most profound example of this resurgence of pride in Moses is the incident regarding water coming from a rock.

Numbers 20 recounts another occurrence of Israel grumbling against Moses because of the lack of water. A parallel, but distinct, event occurred earlier in Moses' life (Ex. 17:1–7). Now the Israelites were at it again.

> If only we had died when our brothers fell dead before the LORD! Why did you bring the LORD's community into this wilderness, that we and our livestock should die here? Why did you bring us up out of Egypt to this terrible place? It has no grain or figs, grapevines or pomegranates. And there is no water to drink! (Num. 20:3–5)

Moses had grown accustomed to this type of complaining and he knew where to take the needs of the people. He and Aaron approached God at the tabernacle to seek his assistance. God responded to their request and instructed Moses as follows: "Take the staff, and you and your brother Aaron gather the assembly together. Speak to that rock before their eyes and it will pour out its water. You will bring water out of the rock for the community so they and their livestock can drink" (Num. 20:8).

Moses and Aaron assembled Israel together to once again display for them the power and provision of the Lord. But Moses made a crucial mistake. He likely made it in frustration and haste, but he made it nonetheless. You can feel his displeasure and frustration with the people of Israel in the way he addressed them, "Listen, you rebels" (Num. 20:10). But then, as he continued, he made his great mistake, "Must *we* bring you water out of this rock?" (Num. 20:10). And then he struck the rock twice with his rod (Num. 20:11).

Although scholars have debated the exact nature of Moses' sin here, it seems that the core of his error was in appropriating to himself that which was exclusively attributable to God. Perhaps we have a hint of this in his use of the plural pronoun "we" in Numbers 20:10, whereby Moses includes himself in the same class as God. But we clearly see him overstepping his bounds by failing to follow God's explicit instructions. God told Moses to "speak to the rock," but Moses instead decided to strike the rock twice.

Moses once again allowed his pride to lead him to presume too much. He ignored God's precise instructions and substituted in its place his own interpretation. Old Testament scholar Martin Emmrich summarizes well the core of Moses' sin in this account; "Moses' sin consisted in failing to glorify God by performing the miracle precisely according to Yahweh's instructions."[1] This really is at the heart of every sin from the sin of our first parents right down to every sin we commit today. It is the sin of autonomy whereby we substitute our own judgment in the place of God's judgment and replace God's ultimate authority with our own.

Because this sin was so grave, God declared an equally grave punishment upon Moses. "Because you did not trust in me enough to honor me as holy in the sight of the Israelites, you will not bring this community into the land I give them" (Num. 20:12). God prohibited Moses from entering the land of promise. Some may think this an overly harsh judgment against Moses, perhaps viewing it as out of proportion to the crime, particularly given Moses' many years of faithful service. But we must remember the unique role Moses had and his access to God. The words of Leviticus 10:3, which God declared through Moses and Aaron, come to mind: "Among those who approach me I will be proved holy; in the sight of all the people I will be honored." Moses failed to do this and he paid dearly for it.

This sin of Moses serves an important role in regard to Moses' relationship to Jesus Christ. It is much like that of David's adultery with Bathsheba and his murder of Uriah. These sins in the lives of such great Old Testament figures serve to distinguish them from Jesus Christ. Moses was a great mediator and prophet and David was a great king, but they both were sinners like you and me. Only Jesus, as our prophet, priest, and king, can also serve as the perfect sacrifice for sin. Unlike Moses and David, Jesus was without sin and never failed to honor his Father or keep his Word. Jesus never substituted his will for that of his Father; his cry was always, "Not my will, but yours be done" (Luke 22:42).

A SUCCESSION PLAN (NUMBERS 27)

The final part of Moses' story flows directly from his grave sin against God recorded in Numbers 20. Because Moses could not enter the land of promise, a new leader was needed to complete this task. Moses understood this need.

In Numbers 27, God told Moses to climb a mountain so that he could see the land of promise that he could not enter (Num. 27:12). God again explained to Moses why he was prohibited from entering with the people. At this point, Moses did not complain or plead his case. Instead, like a great leader would, he voiced concern over who would succeed him in leadership:

> May the LORD, the God who gives breath to all living things, appoint someone over this community to go out and come in before them, one who will lead them out and bring them in, so the LORD's people will not be like sheep without a shepherd. (Num. 27:16–17)

Moses' concern was not for himself, but for the people.

Succession planning is a major concern for most businesses. It often goes very poorly. In my own experience in the legal world, I have seen many succession disasters. Most of these disasters occurred because there really was no succession plan. The reason for the absence of the plan is that the person who was to be succeeded simply wasn't able to be selfless; he or she was too focused on his or her own self-importance and financial interests rather than on the needs of the firm. Moses wasn't like that. He could have been and we all would have understood his hurt feelings, but he simply wasn't like that. His sole concern was for the people of Israel, the very same people who had constantly criticized his leadership.

God heard Moses' cry for succession and he provided Joshua to succeed him (Num. 27:18). God then provided instructions on how to anoint Joshua as Moses' successor (Num. 27:18–21). This time Moses followed God's word to the letter. "Moses did as the LORD commanded him" (Num. 27:22).

To me the end of Moses' life and ministry is one of his best and most glorious moments. He ended well. He set aside his personal pride and glory and sought only the best for his people and to fulfill the will of the Lord. In doing so, Moses once again foreshadowed the Lord Jesus. Recall Moses' concern for his people; he was concerned that they have a leader "so the LORD's people will not be like sheep without a shepherd" (Num. 27:17). Jesus had a similar concern for the lost. He gives voice to this in Matthew 9:36: "When he saw the crowds, he had compassion on them, because they were harassed and helpless, like sheep without a shepherd." Likewise, Jesus had a concern for the whole church being without his direct earthly presence in the wake of his death, resurrection, and ascension. Accordingly, Jesus provided his people with the Holy Spirit so that we would not be like sheep without a shepherd. The heart of leadership according to the Scriptures is service. Jesus, of course, is the example of this par excellence. Jesus displayed servant leadership throughout his ministry, from his incarnation, to his washing of the disciples' feet, to his very death on the cross. But Moses also understood servant leadership and in his succession fulfilled the words of Philippians 2:1–4:

> Therefore if you have any encouragement from being united with Christ, if any comfort from his love, if any common sharing in the Spirit, if any tenderness and compassion, then make my joy complete by being like-minded, having the same love, being one in spirit and of one mind. Do nothing out of selfish ambition or vain conceit. Rather, in humility value others above yourselves, not looking to your own interests but each of you to the interests of the others.

As Moses passed the baton of leadership to Joshua, he did it with a servant's heart and the mind of Christ.

MOSES' EPITAPH

As this book closes, I hope that you have caught a glimpse of this extraordinary man of faith named Moses. I concur with the great Reformed biblical theologian Geerhardus Vos, who once remarked of Moses, "No greater name was known in the annals of Old Testament redemption. Prophet, priest, lawgiver in one, he towers high above all others."[2] There is so much to be learned about the Christian life, leadership, and redemption from examining the life of this man. Of course, while Moses does tower above the other figures of the Old Testament, he is eclipsed by the presence of his own Lord and Savior. In fact, Moses' most important role, as I hope you have seen in this book, was to point to Jesus Christ and the redemption that was secured through his work.

Many more things could be said about Moses and his ministry, but thankfully Scripture provides him with an appropriate epitaph in Hebrews 11, and so this book will close with the inspired words of Holy Scripture regarding God's servant Moses:

> By faith Moses, when he had grown up, refused to be known as the son of Pharaoh's daughter. He chose to be mistreated along with the people of God rather than to enjoy the fleeting pleasures of sin. He regarded disgrace for the sake of Christ as of greater value than the treasures of Egypt, because he was looking ahead to his reward. By faith he left Egypt, not fearing the king's anger; he persevered because he saw him who is invisible. By faith he kept the Passover and the application of blood, so that the destroyer of the firstborn would not touch the firstborn of Israel. (Heb. 11:24–28)

FOR FURTHER REFLECTION

1. How was Moses' leadership challenged in Numbers 12? How did Moses' response to this betrayal reveal his Christlikeness?
2. What lesson did Moses have to relearn in Numbers 20? What does this reveal about him? What does it teach us about ourselves?

3. What was the nature of Moses' sin in Numbers 20?
4. What punishment did Moses receive for his sin in Numbers 20? How does Moses' sin and punishment serve to point us to the glory of Jesus Christ?
5. How does the account of Moses' succession by Joshua reveal the leadership qualities and spiritual maturity of Moses?
6. Why does Hebrews 11:24–28 serve as a fitting epitaph for Moses' life?

NOTES

INTRODUCTION
1 Geerhardus Vos, *Biblical Theology: Old and New Testaments* (1948; repr., Edinburgh: Banner of Truth, 1996), 104.

CHAPTER FOUR: WHAT'S IN A NAME?
1 Michael D. Williams, *Far as the Curse Is Found: The Covenant Story of Redemption* (Phillipsburg, NJ: P&R Publishing, 2005), 29.
2 Ibid., 30.

CHAPTER SIX: THE PROPHET, THE PHARAOH, AND THE PLAGUES
1 J. A. Motyer, *The Message of Exodus,* The Bible Speaks Today (Downers Grove, IL: IVP, 2005), 122.
2 Ibid.
3 Ibid.
4 For a helpful discussion and analysis of the theological implications of the hardening of Pharaoh's heart, see G. K. Beale, "An Exegetical and Theological Consideration of the Hardening of Pharaoh's Heart in Exodus 4–14 and Romans 9," *Trinity Journal* 5 NS (1984): 129–54.

CHAPTER NINE: THE LAW CAME THROUGH MOSES
1 Mark Strom, *The Symphony of Scripture: Making Sense of the Bible's Many Themes* (Downers Grove, IL: IVP, 1990), 51.
2 Philip Graham Ryken, *Written in Stone: The Ten Commandments and Today's Moral Crisis* (Wheaton, IL: Crossway, 2003), 66.
3 Although the metaphor of God as a mother is much less dominant in the Scriptures, God also uses this idea to explain his relationship to us (e.g., Matt. 23:37). The use of this type of mother imagery does not change the reality that God does not have gender as we do, nor does it change the reality that God has chosen to reveal himself to us primarily in the masculine gender.

4 There is a longstanding theological debate regarding where the division between these two categories begins. Some (mainly Lutherans and Catholics) contend that the first four commandments deal with our relationship with God and the other six are related to human interaction, while others (the Reformed view) contend that the division should be made after the Fifth Commandment.

5 Graeme Goldsworthy, *According to Plan: The Unfolding Revelation of God in the Bible* (Downers Grove, IL: IVP, 1991), 144.

6 Ibid., 144.

CHAPTER TEN: FROM IDOLATRY TO GLORY

1 We must understand that this verse does not deny the doctrine of the immutability of God's character and will, but rather reflects a withholding of God's judgment based on his compassion and grace.

EPILOGUE

1 Martin Emmrich, "The Case against Moses Reopened," *Journal of the Evangelical Theological Society* 46 (2003): 53.

2 Geerhardus Vos, *Grace and Glory* (1922; rev. ed., Edinburgh: Banner of Truth, 1994), 88.

INDEX OF SCRIPTURE